Sustainability

Series Editor: Cara Acred

Volume 290

Independence Educational Publishers

First published by Independence Educational Publishers

The Studio, High Green

Great Shelford

Cambridge CB22 5EG

England

© Independence 2016

ISBN-13: 9781861687265

Printed in Great Britain
Zenith Print Group

Contents

Chapter 1: Sustainability issues

What is sustainability?	1
Living Planet Report 2014	2
Rate of environmental degradation puts life on Earth at risk, says scientists	4
UK "could run out of land by 2030" as housing, food and energy compete for space	5
Three trillion trees live on Earth, but there would be twice as many without humans	6
What is sustainable food?	7
What makes a sustainable menu?	9
Food for thought	11
Hungry for land: small farmers feed the world with less than a quarter of all farmland	12
World footprint: do we fit on the planet?	14
What is sustainable development?	16
How green is your city? Towards an index of urban sustainability	17
Water for a Sustainable World	18

Chapter 2: Sustainable solutions

It's time to shout stop on this war on the living world	20
Transforming our world: the 2030 Agenda for Sustainable Development	22
How much water is there in your boots?	24
How do we achieve a sustainable lifestyle?	25
Personal contribution to sustainability	29
Grow your own; buy the rest from a wide range of outlets	30
£160-million technology boost for UK agriculture industries	33
Vertical farms offer a bright future for hungry cities	34
Eight ways business is helping to protect the environment	36
Crowd votes with its feet to back tech firm that turns footsteps into electricity	37
Pavegen introduces pedestrian power in UK's most sustainable building!	38

Key facts	40
Glossary	41
Assignments	42
Index	43
Acknowledgements	44

Introduction

Sustainability is Volume 290 in the **ISSUES** series. The aim of the series is to offer current, diverse information about important issues in our world, from a UK perspective.

ABOUT SUSTAINABILITY

With our planet's resources dwindling, 'sustainable living' is an increasingly debated topic. In essence, sustainability is about balancing our lifestyle with Earth's resources to keep the environment healthy and minimise our impact. This book looks at both issues and solutions, exploring our consumption of natural resources such as food, land and water. It also looks at how we can achieve a sustainable lifestyle, considering innovations for a sustainable future such as vertical farms and electricity-generating pavements!

OUR SOURCES

Titles in the **ISSUES** series are designed to function as educational resource books, providing a balanced overview of a specific subject.

The information in our books is comprised of facts, articles and opinions from many different sources, including:

⇨ Newspaper reports and opinion pieces

⇨ Website factsheets

⇨ Magazine and journal articles

⇨ Statistics and surveys

⇨ Government reports

⇨ Literature from special interest groups

A NOTE ON CRITICAL EVALUATION

Because the information reprinted here is from a number of different sources, readers should bear in mind the origin of the text and whether the source is likely to have a particular bias when presenting information (or when conducting their research). It is hoped that, as you read about the many aspects of the issues explored in this book, you will critically evaluate the information presented.

It is important that you decide whether you are being presented with facts or opinions. Does the writer give a biased or unbiased report? If an opinion is being expressed, do you agree with the writer? Is there potential bias to the 'facts' or statistics behind an article?

ASSIGNMENTS

In the back of this book, you will find a selection of assignments designed to help you engage with the articles you have been reading and to explore your own opinions. Some tasks will take longer than others and there is a mixture of design, writing and research-based activities that you can complete alone or in a group.

FURTHER RESEARCH

At the end of each article we have listed its source and a website that you can visit if you would like to conduct your own research. Please remember to critically evaluate any sources that you consult and consider whether the information you are viewing is accurate and unbiased.

Useful weblinks

www.theconversation.com

www.foe.co.uk

www.footprintnetwork.org

www.gov.uk

www.grain.org

www.greatbusinessdebate.co.uk

www.theguardian.com

www.imeche.org

www.pavegen.com

www.populationmatters.org

www.sd-commission.org.uk

www.sustainablefoodtrust.org

www.sustainweb.org

www.thetelegraph.co.uk

en.unesco.org

www.wwf.org.uk

What is sustainability?

Living sustainably means balancing our consumption, our technology choices and our population numbers in order to live within the resources of the planet. It means maintaining a stable and healthy environment for both humanity and biodiversity.

The implications are radical. As a minimum a sustainable society, i.e. one that could physically be sustained indefinitely, would need a stable or reducing population, very high levels of reuse and recycling, 100% renewable energy and no net loss of soil and biodiversity. No country is yet near it.

We are already eating into our capital, collectively consuming the renewable resources of 1.5 planets, according to the respected World Wildlife Fund/Global Footprint Network *Living Planet Report*.

There are no magic numbers, only trade-offs. Any given area of land can sustain many more very low-consuming poor people at bare subsistence than it can very high-consuming rich people living like millionaires. Better technology always helps; but basically, the richer we all become, the fewer of us the planet, or any country in it, can sustain; and the more of us there are, the lower our sustainable standard of living will be.

The choice is fewer who are richer, or more who are poorer.

Population Matters seeks an optimal balance, offering the best quality of life, not the greatest quantity of possessions. This implies modest but reasonably comfortable standards of living free from hunger or insecurity, which enables fulfilment without increasing physical consumption. Only non-physical things – like quality of relationships, intelligence, education, knowledge, skills, health, arts, spiritual growth, respect, fun – can increase indefinitely in a physically finite world.

Sustainable business and governmental policies would ensure the take-up of renewable energy and material sources while phasing out those with adverse side effects. Increased effort is needed to minimise waste of energy, water, food and other commodities. In a finite world even renewable resources are only available in limited quantities.

Halting population growth and in many countries reversing it, is a vital part of living sustainably. In some societies, population growth has already slowed or stopped. Typically, the empowerment of women and improved availability of contraception have played major roles.

Compared with the challenge of asking people to reduce their living standards or change the fundamental technological basis of their society, approaches seeking a reduced birth rate are low cost and proven. The unborn people who never existed, and all their non-existent descendants in perpetuity, have no impact on our planet.

Gradually reducing our numbers back to the levels of one or two generations ago is one of the best ways of addressing the environmental and resource challenges we face.

What does sustainability look like?

An activity that is sustainable is one that is capable of continuing indefinitely. The conflict between this and the fact that the world is finite is often overlooked, leading to the term 'sustainable' being widely abused. Growth, for example, can never be truly sustainable so 'sustainable growth' is a contradiction in terms.

People rely on a number of resources and a healthy environment if they are to prosper. Since the first appearance of mankind, we have sometimes used resources unsustainably, but in the distant past, due to the then relatively low levels of our population, the impact was usually only local, or at worst regional. Since the Industrial Revolution, on the other hand, human activity and impact on the environment have grown relentlessly. We are now using many resources on an industrially

The resources we use and our impact on the environment effectively depend on three main factors:

- Population – how many of us there are consuming and creating waste

- Affluence, or consumption – the amount of goods and services on average we each use

- Technology – how inefficiently/harmfully we produce these goods and services

intensive scale and much faster than they can be replenished, thereby causing irreparable damage to the environment.

In the natural world, species that live unsustainably, exceeding the carrying capacity of their environment by exhausting resources and degrading the environment, eventually experience a rapid and often catastrophic crash in numbers. If we don't take measures to prevent it, sooner or later this will happen to us, but it doesn't need to be that way.

Excessive levels of personal consumption and inefficient or polluting technology are obviously unsustainable. But even the best technology and the most modest life styles will still have some effect on the environment. This means that, if the population keeps on growing, human activity will inevitably become unsustainable. To assure a good or even acceptable quality of life in the future, it is essential that we humans ensure that all three factors (Affluence, Technology and Population) are attended to.

On the other hand, so long as no one of the above three factors is too far out of line, there are many different sustainable solutions. Let's suppose that the very best environmentally friendly technology available is put into practice (this is not a foregone conclusion). Sustainable scenarios range from the maximum possible number of people all living at subsistence levels to a much smaller population all living very luxuriously. Provided the total environmental impact and consumption of resources is not excessive, any of these scenarios would be sustainable.

⇨ The above information is reprinted with kind permission from Population Matters. Please visit www.populationmatters.org for further information.

Living Planet Report 2014

An extract from the WWF report.

Biodiversity is declining sharply, while our demands on nature are unsustainable and increasing. Species populations worldwide have declined 52 per cent since 1970. We need 1.5 Earths to meet the demands we currently make on nature. This means we are eating into our natural capital, making it more difficult to sustain the needs of future generations. The dual effect of a growing human population and high per capita footprint will multiply the pressure we place on our resources. Countries with a high level of human development tend to have higher ecological footprints. The challenge is for countries to increase their human development while keeping their footprint down to globally sustainable levels. We may have already crossed 'planetary boundaries' that could lead to abrupt or irreversible environmental changes. Human well-being depends on natural resources such as water, arable land, fish and wood; and ecosystem services such as pollination, nutrient cycling and erosion control. While the world's poorest continue to be more vulnerable, the interconnected issues of food, water and energy security affect us all.

We are all in this together – Foreword by Marco Lambertini, Director General of WWF International

This latest edition of the *Living Planet Report* is not for the faint-hearted. One key point that jumps out is that the Living Planet Index (LPI), which measures more than 10,000 representative populations of mammals, birds, reptiles, amphibians and fish, has declined by 52 per cent since 1970. Put another way, in less than two human generations, population sizes of vertebrate species have dropped by half. These are the living forms that constitute the fabric of the ecosystems which sustain life on Earth – and the barometer of what we are doing to our own planet, our only home. We ignore their decline at our peril.

We have to remind ourselves that this is 'progress'.

How are our consumption levels affecting biodiversity and endangered species?

Source: WWF Living PLanet Report, Human Impact, 2013

We are all connected – and collectively, we have the potential to find and adopt the solutions that will safeguard the future of this, our one and only planet.

Why we should care

For many, planet Earth and the staggering web of life to which we all belong are worth protecting for their own sake. A sense of wonder and a profound respect for nature runs deep in many cultures and religions. People instinctively relate to the well-known proverb: We do not inherit the Earth from our ancestors; we borrow it from our children. Yet we are not proving good stewards of our one planet. The way we meet our needs today is compromising the ability of future generations to meet theirs – the very opposite of sustainable development.

Humanity's well-being and prosperity – indeed, our very existence – depends on healthy ecosystems and the services they supply, from clean water and a liveable climate, to food, fuel, fibre and fertile soils. Progress has been made in recent years in quantifying the financial value of this natural capital and the dividends that flow from it. Such valuations make an economic case for conserving nature and living sustainably – although any valuation of ecosystem services is a "gross underestimate of infinity", since without them there can be no life on Earth.

Published in 2014

⇨ The above information is reprinted with kind permission from the WWF. Please visit www.wwf.org.uk for further information.

We are using nature's gifts as if we had more than just one Earth at our disposal. By taking more from our ecosystems and natural processes than can be replenished, we are jeopardising our very future. Nature conservation and sustainable development go hand-in-hand. They are not only about preserving biodiversity and wild places, but just as much about safeguarding the future of humanity – our well-being, economy, food security and social stability – indeed, our very survival.

In a world where so many people live in poverty, it may appear as though protecting nature is a luxury. But it is quite the opposite. For many of the world's poorest people, it is a lifeline. Importantly though, we are all in this together. We all need nutritious food, fresh water and clean air – wherever in the world we live.

Things look so worrying that it may seem difficult to feel positive about the future. Difficult, certainly, but not impossible – because it is in ourselves, who have caused the problem, that we can find the solution. Now we must work to ensure that the upcoming generation can seize the opportunity that we have so far failed to grasp, to close this destructive chapter in our history, and build a future where people can live and prosper in harmony with nature.

Rate of environmental degradation puts life on Earth at risk, say scientists

Humans are "eating away at our own life support systems" at a rate unseen in the past 10,000 years, two new research papers say.

By Oliver Milman

Humans are "eating away at our own life support systems" at a rate unseen in the past 10,000 years by degrading land and freshwater systems, emitting greenhouse gases and releasing vast amounts of agricultural chemicals into the environment, new research has found.

Two major new studies by an international team of researchers have pinpointed the key factors that ensure a liveable planet for humans, with stark results.

Of nine worldwide processes that underpin life on Earth, four have exceeded "safe" levels – human-driven climate change, loss of biosphere integrity, land system change and the high level of phosphorus and nitrogen flowing into the oceans due to fertiliser use.

Researchers spent five years identifying these core components of a planet suitable for human life, using the long-term average state of each measure to provide a baseline for the analysis.

They found that the changes of the last 60 years are unprecedented in the previous 10,000 years, a period in which the world has had a relatively stable climate and human civilisation has advanced significantly.

Carbon dioxide levels, at 395.5 parts per million, are at historic highs, while loss of biosphere integrity is resulting in species becoming extinct at a rate more than 100 times faster than the previous norm.

Since 1950, urban populations have increased seven-fold, primary energy use has soared by a factor of five, while the amount of fertiliser used is now eight times higher. The amount of nitrogen entering the oceans has quadrupled.

All of these changes are shifting Earth into a "new state" that is becoming less hospitable to human life, researchers said.

"These indicators have shot up since 1950 and there are no signs they are slowing down," said Professor Will Steffen of the Australian National University and the Stockholm Resilience Centre. Steffen is the lead author on both of the studies.

"When economic systems went into overdrive, there was a massive increase in resource use and pollution. It used to be confined to local and regional areas but we're now seeing this occurring on a global scale. These changes are down to human activity, not natural variability."

Steffen said direct human influence upon the land was contributing to a loss in pollination and a disruption in the provision of nutrients and fresh water.

"We are clearing land, we are degrading land, we introduce feral animals and take the top predators out, we change the marine ecosystem by overfishing – it's a death by a thousand cuts," he said. "That direct impact upon the land is the most important factor right now, even more than climate change."

There are large variations in conditions around the world, according to the research. For example, land clearing is now concentrated in tropical areas, such as Indonesia and the Amazon, with the practice reversed in parts of Europe. But the overall picture is one of deterioration at a rapid rate.

"It's fairly safe to say that we haven't seen conditions in the past similar to ones we see today and there is strong evidence that there [are] tipping points we don't want to cross," Steffen said.

"If the Earth is going to move to a warmer state, 5–6°C warmer, with no ice caps, it will do so and that won't be good for large mammals like us. People say the world is robust and that's true, there will be life on Earth, but the Earth won't be robust for us.

"Some people say we can adapt due to technology, but that's a belief system, it's not based on fact. There is no convincing evidence that a large mammal, with a core body temperature of 37°C, will be able to evolve that quickly. Insects can, but humans can't and that's a problem."

Steffen said the research showed the economic system was "fundamentally flawed" as it ignored critically important life support systems.

"It's clear the economic system is driving us towards an unsustainable future and people of my daughter's generation will find it increasingly hard to survive," he said. "History has shown that civilisations have risen, stuck to their core values and then collapsed because they didn't change. That's where we are today."

The two studies, published in *Science* and *Anthropocene Review*, featured the work of scientists from countries including the US, Sweden, Germany and India. The findings will be presented in seven seminars at the World Economic Forum in Davos, which takes place between 21 and 25 January.

15 January 2015

⇨ The above information is reprinted with kind permission from *The Guardian*. Please visit www.theguardian.com for further information.

UK "could run out of land by 2030" as housing, food and energy compete for space

Space required for new housing, energy, food and environmental projects could leave a potential land shortfall three times the size of Wales, Cambridge University study warns.

By Emily Gosden

The UK could run out of land to meet its growing demands for food, housing, green energy and environmental protection by 2030, according to a Cambridge University-backed report.

There could be a shortfall of as much as six million hectares of land – three times the size of Wales – to meet the requirements of a series of policy aims as Britain's population grows, the study found.

It warned there was a "worrying lack of clarity" from government about how much agricultural land was expected to be repurposed to fulfil its various policy goals.

The report said that between two million and seven million hectares of further agricultural land could potentially be needed for housing, further woodland, crops for biofuels, crops to increase Britain's

food security, and dedicated areas to protect wildlife.

"With the UK population forecast to reach 71.4 million by 2030 from 62.6 million in 2012, the additional demands for food, living, working and amenity space will create further, significant pressures on land," it said.

"New residential and commercial developments, transport infrastructure, food production, environmental needs and recreational space will be competing for land."

However, only between one million and five million hectares of such land could potentially be freed up, through more efficient farming, reductions in food wastage and by people switching to eat less meat, which is land-intensive to produce.

This could therefore leave a shortfall of as much as six million hectares if demand grows in line with the highest scenarios and supply increases in line with the lowest.

Andrew Montague-Fuller, programme manager at the Cambridge Institute for Sustainability Leadership which produced the report, said: "In this initial analysis, we identified a significant gap between additional land demand and potential supply, as well as a worrying lack of clarity about what agricultural land is expected to deliver.

"It is clear that more research is needed, and that business, government, farmers and landowners need to work together to

ensure we can meet these growing demands, while also protecting the environment."

A spokesman for the Department of Energy and Climate Change said: "DECC recognises that land resources are limited, and there could be increased competition between land used for agriculture, living space, energy, nature and ecosystem services in the future. We agree with the report's conclusions that land should be used more efficiently in future – for example, agricultural residues and manures used for energy generation, crop yields increased, and food waste minimised."

A Defra spokesperson said: "We have good food security in the UK thanks to our own thriving £97.1 billion food and farming industry and trade access to markets across the globe. We are investing £70 million in agricultural technologies that will help us to increase the efficiency of food production and help our food, farming and science industries grow economically while meeting the increasing global demand for food."

25 June 2014

⇨ The above information is reprinted with kind permission from *The Telegraph*. Please visit www.telegraph.co.uk for further information.

Three trillion trees live on Earth, but there would be twice as many without humans

An article from The Conversation.

THE CONVERSATION

By James Dyke, Lecturer in Complex Systems Simulation, University of Southampton

Each year, humans reduce the number of trees worldwide by 15 billion. This is one of the startling conclusions of new research published in the journal *Nature*. The study also estimates the Earth is home to more than three trillion trees – that's 3,000 billion – so you may think that while 15 billion is a very large number, humans shouldn't be at risk of making significant changes to global tree cover.

However, the team of 31 international scientists led by Thomas Crowther at Yale University also present evidence that the rise of human civilisation has reduced the numbers of trees on Earth by 46%. In many areas we can't see the wood because there are no trees. Unlike polar bears, pandas or peregrine falcons, trees and their demise typically do not generate much passion or protest. But the 180,000km^2 of tree cover being lost each year represents a serious destabilising force on the current biosphere.

Previous estimates for the total number of trees on Earth have been much lower. The new study is important not only because it gives a higher number, but how it was produced. As well as using remote sensing data such as images taken by satellites that can classify land type, the research also integrated 429,775 ground-based assessments of tree density.

The researchers used this information to build a series of mathematical models which can fill in any gaps in the data with robust estimates. This allowed them to produce the first continuous map of global tree densities at the one square kilometre scale.

Humans have long used trees as fuel for cooking or smelting, fibres

for clothes, timber for construction. However, it is the indirect value of trees that may prove to be more important.

A solitary tree can provide a habitat to myriad species in its leaves, branches, bark and roots. But it is the effects trees have on their environments that can affect life across entire landscapes. When alive, trees can stabilise slopes and the course of rivers and streams. When dead their wood debris can form dams and so create ponds and lakes.

As well as changing water on the ground, they can alter it in the air. Transpiration is the name given to the process whereby trees (and other plants) suck up water through their roots, transport it through trunks and branches leaving the tree through tiny holes called stoma in their leaves. Stoma are crucial as they allow carbon dioxide to be absorbed, which along with water and sunlight are the ingredients with which all trees produce their food.

Only a fraction of the water absorbed is consumed during photosynthesis, with the rest evaporating out from leaf stoma. This means some trees act as massive humidifiers. Through sucking up water held in soil and releasing it tens of metres above the ground, forests can be effective cloud machines as that water vapour rises and then condenses. This is one of the reasons why it rains in the rainforest.

Global impacts of tree loss

As well as changing local weather, large forests can affect the global climate. Through the burning of fossil fuels, humans release approximately 32 billion tons of carbon dioxide into the atmosphere, each year. Higher concentrations of CO_2 in the air can

lead to faster rates of photosynthesis and more vigorous tree and plant growth, a process termed carbon fertilisation. This draws some of this additional carbon dioxide back down from the atmosphere. The Amazon rainforest alone absorbs approximately two billion tons of extra carbon dioxide each year. Within its leaves, branches, trunks and roots lies more than a 100 billion metric tonnes of carbon. Thus the Amazon rainforest has served as an important counter to anthropogenic climate change.

Rather worryingly, it appears as if the Amazon's ability to soak up excessive carbon dioxide is grinding to a halt. Faster tree growth has been accompanied with higher mortality. Trees that live fast die young. As climate change progresses, mortality rates are predicted to climb higher largely as a consequence of extreme weather events such as droughts. A world that continues to warm is one which could see a significantly reduced Amazon rain forest.

The dieback of the Amazon has been identified as a potential global tipping point. There are good reasons to think that the Amazon rainforest, if sufficiently stressed by climate change could rapidly collapse and be replaced by savannah-type vegetation or even desert. After all, less than 10,000 years ago the Sahara was lush and well populated. Any appreciable dieback of the Amazon would lead to many billions of tons of carbon dioxide being added to the atmosphere as the carbon previously locked up in tree biomass is released as dead wood decomposes.

The Amazon drought of 2010 greatly increased tree mortality with the result that more than two billion tons of carbon dioxide was emitted into the Earth's atmosphere (that's four times as much as the UK's contribution in 2012). Over mere decades the Amazon could turn from a large sink of carbon to a large source, further amplifying climate change.

A sensible course of action when dealing with this potential carbon bomb would be to reduce our emissions of greenhouse gasses and manage the forest on the ground as best we can. Instead, emissions continue to rise while we hit the unexploded ordinance with a hammer. Or rather a chainsaw.

Trees in the Amazon continue to be felled. Humans are attacking the forest on two fronts: a local front that follows new roads which open up previously undisturbed forest to logging, and a global front through emissions of greenhouse gasses from industrialised nations. The two will interact which could significantly increase the risk of widespread dieback of the Amazon.

The new research published in *Nature* will help improve our understanding of the role trees play in ecological and biogeochemical processes not just in the Amazon but across the globe. This knowledge could help inform management practices for the remaining forests. But perhaps its greatest impact will be the realisation that the emergence of civilisation has led to the net destruction of nearly three trillion of Earth's trees. That could serve as a powerful perspective for comprehending the impacts humans have had on the natural world.

2 September 2015

⇨ The above information is reprinted with kind permission from *The Conversation*. Please visit www.theconversation.com for further information.

What is sustainable food?

There is no legal definition of 'sustainable food,' although some aspects, such as the terms organic or Fairtrade, are clearly defined.

Our working definition for good food is that it should be produced, processed, distributed and disposed of in ways that:

⇨ Contribute to thriving local economies and sustainable livelihoods – both in the UK and, in the case of imported products, in producer countries;

⇨ Protect the diversity of both plants and animals and the welfare of farmed and wild species,

⇨ Avoid damaging or wasting natural resources or contributing to climate change;

⇨ Provide social benefits, such as good quality food, safe and healthy products, and educational opportunities.

Good food

What we mean by good food can be summed up by our seven principles:

1) Aiming to be waste-free

Reducing food waste (and packaging) saves the energy, effort and natural resources used to produce and dispose of it, as well as money.

2) Eating better, and less meat and dairy

Consuming more vegetables and fruit, grains and pulses, and smaller amounts of animal products produced to high-welfare and environmental standards helps reduce health risks and greenhouse gases.

3) Buying local, seasonal and environmentally friendly food

This benefits wildlife and the countryside, minimises the energy used in food production, transport and storage, and helps protect the local economy.

4) Choosing Fairtrade-certified products

This scheme for food and drinks imported from poorer countries ensures a fair deal for disadvantaged producers.

5) Selecting fish only from sustainable sources

Future generations will be able to eat fish and seafood if we act now to protect our rivers and seas and the creatures living there.

6) Getting the balance right

We need to cut down on sugar, salt and fat, and most of us want to avoid questionable ingredients and processes such as genetic modification (GM) and some additives.

7) Growing our own, and buying the rest from a wide range of outlets

Fresh out of the garden or allotment is unbeatable, and a vibrant mix of local markets, small shops and cafés, and other retailers provides choice, variety and good livelihoods.

You've got better food, now...

What's the problem?

Sustainability is not just about the food you eat. Three areas of special concern are dealt with briefly in this article: waste, energy and water. Whilst Sustain does not specialise in advice on these important aspects of the food system, we mention them here because they play an important part in the overall sustainability of our food and farming systems.

Waste

However much energy has been used to make food and its packaging, all of it is wasted when it is thrown away. For example, in the UK we throw away an estimated 6.7 million tonnes of food every year, accounting for around a third of all of the food we buy. About half of this is edible, with the rest comprising of peelings, meat bones and so on. Food also makes up a high proportion of the waste from manufacturing, catering and retail outlets. Fruit, vegetables and salads make up about 19% of the waste by weight from supermarkets. Artificially high cosmetic standards stipulated by supermarkets and caterers can also result in large amounts of a fruit crop going to waste.[1]

Energy

Large amounts of energy are also used to prepare food – in cooking and refrigeration – and indirectly in the production, processing and transporting of the food. Most of this energy will be from non-renewable fossil fuels, and are therefore a significant source of greenhouse gases. In total, the food sector is estimated to be responsible for between 20 and 30 per cent of the UK's greenhouse gas emissions.[2] Much more could be done to improve energy efficiency at home and in food businesses, so that we can all play our part in reducing the greenhouse gas emissions that lead to global warming.

Water

Water demand has increased dramatically over the past quarter of a century, and we now use half as much water again as we did in 1980.[3] This is a result of changes in lifestyles and many more water-using appliances. The need for us to use water more efficiently is due to several factors – not simply because water resources are finite (a good enough reason in itself!). For example, water purification is a major user of energy, which contributes to climate change. In itself, climate change means we can expect hotter, drier summers and more unpredictable weather, with greater risk of droughts and water shortages. We should all do our bit to use water more wisely.

1 Friends of the Earth (2002) Briefing Paper: Supermarkets and Great British fruit, see: http://www. foe.co.uk/resource/briefings/supermarket_british_fruit. pdf

2 Calculations from, for example: Garnett, T., Food Climate Research Network, presentation to Sustain: The alliance for better food and farming, spring 2007. See the FCRN website at: http://www.fcrn.org.uk/, and EIPRO Environmental Impact of Products, April 2005, European Science and Technology Observatory and Institute for Prospective Technological Studies, see: http://ec.europa.eu/environment/ipp/pdf/eipro_ draft_report2.pdf

3 Greater London Authority (2007) Water matters: The Mayor's Draft Water Strategy. See: http://www.london. gov.uk/mayor/environment/water/docs/la-draft-water-strategy.rtf

What can we do about it?

A recent survey from the market research organisation Mintel[4] reported that 71% of British adults recycle as much packaging waste as they can. This attitude is supported by a 2007 government survey, which also showed that around two-thirds of us are concerned about saving energy, and over half about saving water.[5] For example, you can:

⇨ Cut down the amount of excess packaging that comes around your food, by telling retailers that you would prefer to receive goods in minimal packaging. Ask them to explore using packaging that is re-usable, refillable or made from recyclable materials.

⇨ Buy in bulk. Weight for weight, larger boxes, cartons and bags use less packaging materials than smaller ones.

⇨ Choose goods that are (in order of preference):

  • Re-usable – washable crockery, jugs, cutlery and other goods are far better than those that get used only once and then thrown away.

  • Made from recycled materials – to support the market for recycled products.

  • Compostable or recyclable.

⇨ Avoid goods and materials that cannot be re-used, composted or recycled. If it needs to go in the bin, it will go straight to a landfill site, and these are filling up rapidly!

⇨ Cut down food waste you produce by making the very best use of the food you buy, to use up leftovers, and to get creative with what you've got. Putting soup on the family menu is an easy and tasty way to use excess vegetables, and to cater for seasonal variations.

4 Mintel report on Ethical and Green Retailing, June 2007 - to read more go to: http://www.mintel.com/ press_release.php?id=289890

5 Department of the Environment, Food and Rural Affairs (2007) Survey of public attitudes and behaviours towards the environment. http://www. defra.gov.uk/news/2007/070814a.htm

⇨ Participate in a food composting system run by your local authority, or set up a composting pile or worm bin in your garden.

⇨ Don't be fooled by the cosmetic appearance of fruit and vegetables. Use blemished fruit and vegetables and riper fruits that might otherwise go to waste.

⇨ Follow energy and water-saving advice of specialist organisations (see details below).

For further information

Waterwise specialises in providing information about saving water – http://www.waterwise.org.uk/.

UK food waste information is available the Waste Reduction Action Programme (WRAP), at: http://www. lovefoodhatewaste.com/.

Information about composting can be found at http://www. lovefoodhatewaste.com/ and information about worm bins can be found at: http://www.wigglywigglers. co.uk/.

Tips on energy saving are offered by the Energy Savings Trust, see: http:// www.energysavingtrust.org.uk/what_ can_i_do_today/cheap_and_simple_ tips.

Tips on saving water are offered by the Water Guide, see: http://www. water-guide.org.uk/tips.html.

About Sustain

Sustain: The alliance for better food and farming advocates food and agriculture policies and practices that enhance the health and welfare of people and animals, improve the working and living environment, enrich society and culture and promote equity. We represent around 100 national public interest organisations working at international, national, regional and local level. The alliance is a registered charity (no. 1018643) and company limited by guarantee (no. 02673194).

⇨ The above information is reprinted with kind permission from Sustain. For further information visit www.sustainweb.org.

© Sustain 2015

What makes a sustainable menu?

The 'eatwell plate' of the Food Standards Agency has guided food choices since the 1990s, but it has recently come under scrutiny as sustainable food consumption moves up the agenda. With eating out an important part of our culture, how can the catering sector join the debate and put sustainability on the menu?

By Sophie Laggan

This was a key question for the Sustainable Food Summit, held this May in Bristol. Now in its second year, the event brought together a wide spectrum of industry representatives, food-based organisations and myself – a researcher in sustainable food systems – for three hours of productive discussions and workshops tailored to the restaurant trade. With UK consumers' expenditure on catering services totalling £83.9 billion in 2013, the environmental footprint of the farm-to-restaurant supply chain deserves our attention.

For chefs Tim Maddams and Arthur Potts Dawson, who spoke at the event, sustainability has become their moral imperative. On a sustainability crusade, they advocate farm-to-fork thinking for a successful business and personal life. Both gave passionate speeches on how, in recognising that their impact really does make a difference to diners, they were able to make important changes in the dining experience.

Maddams talked of novel ways to conceptualise a menu, be that in sourcing 'incidental meat' such as pigeon, or including under-utilised mutton and offal. They argued that the move to sustainable consumption should really be seen as an opportunity. Diners like novelty, and they are more likely to try something new in a restaurant than during their weekly shop. Diners provide a fertile testing ground for chefs to explore both environmental and economic gains, which encourages a growing consciousness around food production and consumption. Sourcing food locally, for instance, promotes the local economy and shortens supply chains. In turn, this

leads to fewer food miles and also a good talking point over dinner.

Maddams' sustainable plate extends beyond the food on it to include how the restaurant runs. Just because your beef is grass fed and the samphire foraged with your own bare hands, you are not let off leaving the tap running or the oven door open. At the scale of industrial kitchens, this really does make a difference, but for individuals too, small changes accumulate into a significant impact.

The day was a refreshing departure from discussions on the health impacts of food – while health is undeniably important, a holistic perspective is needed on the sustainable plate. And this is very much reflected in the changing face of what British people see as a typical meal.

Why menus look the way they do

Wartime rationing prescribed fair distribution of food and a surge in homegrown produce during the 1940s. We should not forget the 'dig for victory' propaganda that is making a well-deserved

comeback! However, it was not until the 1970s that a guideline for how to eat was developed Europe.

Gripped by high food prices, Sweden created a food pyramid detailing the 'correct' servings of foods, from breads and cereals to fats and oils. It was intended to offer "good wholesome food at reasonable prices". No health claims were made.

The US Department of Agriculture (USDA) adapted the food pyramid for its market shortly after. Heavy lobbying from the food industry had a significant influence on the types and amounts of food that appeared on this version. As nutritionist Luise Light, former USDA insider, explains:

"Where we, the USDA nutritionists, called for a base of five to nine servings of fresh fruits and vegetables a day, it was replaced with a paltry two to three servings… changes were made to the wording of the dietary guidelines from 'eat less' to 'avoid too much', giving a nod to the processed food industry interests by not limiting highly profitable 'fun foods' (junk foods by any other name) that might affect the bottom line of food companies."

"For the first time in 20 years, the eatwell plate has been given a makeover"

Similarly, Britain's 'eatwell plate', developed in 1994, was also subject to industry lobbying; you only have to look at the Kellogg's box that appears in some versions to see the blatant influence. Alternative 'healthy eating' plates are out there, such as My Vegan Plate, although this still suggests between six and 11 servings of carbohydrates, which by some accounts is too high.

Proposals for sustainable eating

For the first time in 20 years, the eatwell plate has been given a makeover. The World Wildlife Fund have proposed a Livewell 2020 Diet, which sees an increase in vegetable consumption by two per cent and a decrease in 'non-dairy protein' to balance the plate. It calculates the relative contribution to greenhouse gas (GHG) emissions for each slice of the pie and offers a useful model around which to base menus – one that is based on exploration and experimentation. However, the Livewell Diet still suffers from some of the same flaws as its predecessors, and foods high in fat and sugar have even increased. Further, neither locality nor seasonality is mentioned in the Livewell Diet. So, while embedded GHG emissions can be reduced by 25% if we all adopt this diet, it is, again, far from a holistic picture of sustainable eating.

A 2008 study calculated that even if reducing food miles to zero was achievable, the savings on this for GHG emissions would only equate to 5% – the equivalent of driving just 1,000 fewer miles a year. By comparison, one meat and dairy free day per week would save 1,160 miles. In cutting back on meat, diners begin opening their minds to alternatives and thinking differently

about their food. It can be a unique selling point for caterers.

Friends of the Earth (FOE) propose the 'Flexitarian' diet, which is defined as mainly plant based, but allows small amounts of meat, fish and dairy. FOE have ambitions of making Bristol into Britain's first Flexitarian city. The average daily water consumption of a meat-eating person is 5,000 litres per day: the average vegetarian uses half of this. So with drought predicted to become more frequent in the future as a result of climate change, we need to evaluate more carefully the impact on our water resources of how we eat.

Another novel idea, which Luke Hasell, farmer and director of Eat Drink Bristol Fashion, is championing, is increasing the age of slaughter for farm animals. In doing so diners will not only have a tastier morsel to savour, they will reduce the need to house so many animals: tender cuts of meat require that animals move less and are thus kept in confinement, raising animal welfare issues. It's a no brainer really: the diner leaves satisfied and the welfare of the animal is improved.

Nothing goes to waste

Food is wasted at each step of the supply chain: it remains unpicked if it is 'ugly'; it perishes over long distances; it is 'trimmed' for aesthetics; and it is left on the plate of not-so-hungry customers. Caterers have the ability to intercept at each of these junctures. They can champion crooked carrots, source local food in season, use peelings for stocks and offer different portion sizes. And when waste remains, they can donate surplus to food waste charities such as Foodcycle. At the Sustainable Food Summit, Dawson even went so far as to say "why give diners so much choice?" And why not provide just one or two options? It is a bold statement but perhaps a necessary one.

Building a brand

Citing a regionally sourced product on the menu adds value and interest. "Diners can take

food home and talk about it," says Maddams. The Bristol Fish Project could be one promising way to push sustainable alternatives of fish production, for instance, as could the local branding scheme Eat Bristol, which the civil society-led Food Policy Council is currently in the process of developing. If the project is implemented, Eat Bristol could help to increase the market for local produce and raise the profile of growers in the region.

To stay ahead of the game, caterers should jump on the bandwagon and create a culture around sustainable food and regional produce. It is better for business as shorter supply chains increase the value of the product and help to build lasting relationships with suppliers, and it is definitely better for the planet. This was the take-home message from the Sustainable Food Summit and although it remains to be seen what impact it will have on the catering trade, it had a lasting impression on me. I'm off to champion farmers and find out what sustainability means to them. We have a lot to learn from the farmers up and down this country and I see this as the first logical step for caterers looking to improve the sustainability of their business model. Sourcing from around the region gives caterers seasonal options to choose from, and the guarantee of quality and a sustainable product to be proud of. To quote Phil Haughton, from the Better Food Company, "We need to get married to our suppliers." Here's hoping caterers tie the knot soon.

29 May 2015

⇨ The above information is reprinted with kind permission from the Sustainable Food Trust. Please visit www.sustainablefoodtrust.org for further information.

© Sustainable Food Trust 2015

FOOD FOR THOUGHT

Current situation

Human health

It is estimateed **half** the population in Europe is obese or overweight

1.5 billion worldwide are overweight

0.87 billion worldwide undernourished

Climate change

Producing pork and chicken creates vastly more carbon dioxide than producing potatoes

In Europe, food accounts for 29% of greenhouse gas emissions

Biodiversity

Agriculture is both a contributor to **biodiversity conservation** and a major driver of **biodiversity loss** much of the land now used for agriculture was once habitat for wildlife

The grassland butterfly population in Europe has massively declined

Land-use & deforestation

European consumption of crops for feed, and pastures for grazing, led to the loss of at least **5.2** million hectares of forests between 1990 and 2008 – an area of land almost twice the size of **Belgium**

We produce enough to feed seven billion people, however...

One third of food produced for human consumption is lost or wasted

The total per capita protein consumption in Europe is about 70% higher than recommended by nutritional guidelines

30% of croplands are used for livestock feed production

25kg is the average per capita consumption of meat in developing countries

25kg

Over 441 million people could have been fed for a year by the amount of food used as fuel in 68 countries

85.1kg is the average per capita consumption of meat in Europe

85.1kg

Benefits of a sustainable diet

Climate

Low-carbon healthier diets could help achieve a **25%** reduction in greenhouse gas emissions from the EU food supply chain in line with EU targets

Water

Following a healthy diet would reduce the EU's current water footprint by 23%

Global food security

According to the UK House of Commons' International Development Committee campaigns to reduce food waste and promote meat as an occasional item – rather than an everyday staple – would have a significant impact on global food security

Public health

In the EU, the estimated costs associated with being overweight or obese vary from **1–5%** of national health care budgets

*** Food cost ***

During tough economic times, the switch to a healthy low-carbon diet will have the added bonus of a reduction in food costs – the adoption of a low-carbon diet would cut a typical French household's food costs by almost £150 a year

Possible solutions

European institutions have acknowledged there needs to be a reduction in global **greenhouse gas emissions** – the principle cause of climate change

The target in the EU's Climate and Energy policy is to cut emissions by at least **20%** below 1990 levels by 2020

80% of respondents indicate that they'd be willing to eat less but better meat

80% of Europeans are concerned about the environmental impact of products

50% say they'd be willing to replace most of the meat they eat with vegetables

Source: Food for Thought, by LiveWell for LIFE. LiveWell for LIFE was a partnership between WWF and Friends of Europe. The project was funded with the contribution of the EU's LIFE+ Programme for the Environment.

Hungry for land: small farmers feed the world with less than a quarter of all farmland

I t is commonly heard today that small farmers produce most of the world's food. But how many of us realise that they are doing this with less than a quarter of the world's farmland, and that even this meagre share is shrinking fast? If small farmers continue to lose the very basis of their existence, the world will lose its capacity to feed itself.

GRAIN took an in-depth look at the data to see what is going on and the message is crystal clear. We need to urgently put land back in the hands of small farmers and make the struggle for agrarian reform central to the fight for better food systems.

Governments and international agencies frequently boast that small farmers control the largest share of the world's agricultural land. Inaugurating 2014 as the International Year of Family Farming, José Graziano da Silva, Director

General of the United Nations Food and Agriculture Organization (FAO), sang the praises of family farmers but didn't once mention the need for land reform. Instead he stated that family farms already manage most of the world's farmland – a whopping 70%, according to his team. Another report published by various UN agencies in 2008 concluded that small farms occupy 60% of all arable land worldwide. Other studies have come to similar conclusions.

But if most of the world's farmland is in small farmers' hands, then why are so many of their organisations clamouring for land redistribution and agrarian reform? Because rural peoples' access to land is under attack everywhere. From Honduras to Kenya and from Palestine to the Philippines, people are being dislodged from their farms and villages. Those who resist are being jailed or killed. Widespread

agrarian strikes in Colombia, protests by community leaders in Madagascar, nationwide marches by landless folk in India, occupations in Andalusia – the list of actions and struggles goes on and on. The bottom line is that land is becoming more and more concentrated in the hands of the rich and powerful, not that small farmers are doing well.

Rural people don't simply make a living off the land, after all. Their land and territories are the backbone of their identities, their cultural landscape and their source of well-being. Yet land is being taken away from them and concentrated in fewer and fewer hands at an alarming pace.

Then there is the other part of the picture: that concerning food. While it is now increasingly common to hear that small farmers produce the majority of the world's food, even if that is outside of market systems, we are also constantly being fed the message that the "more efficient" industrial food system is needed to feed the world. At the same time, we are told that 80% of the world's hungry people live in rural areas, many of them farmers or landless farmworkers.

How do we make sense of all this? What is true and what is not? What action do we take to deal with these imbalances? To help answer some of these questions, GRAIN decided to take a closer look at the facts. We tried to find out how much land is really in the hands of small farmers, and how much food they produce on that land.

The figures and what they tell us

When we looked at the data, we came across quite a number of difficulties. Countries define "small farmer" differently. There are no centralised statistics on who has what land. There are no databases recording how much food comes from where. And different sources give widely varying figures for the amount of agricultural land available in each country.

In compiling the figures, we used official statistics from national agricultural census bureaus in each country wherever possible, complemented by FAOSTAT (FAO's statistical database) and other FAO sources where necessary. For statistical guidance on what a "small farm" is, we generally used the definition provided by each national authority, since the conditions of small farms in different countries and regions can vary widely. Where national definitions were not available, we used the World Bank's criteria.

In light of this, there are important limitations to the data – and our compilation and assessment of them. The dataset that we produced is fully referenced and publicly available online and forms an integral part of this report.

Despite the inherent shortcomings of the data, we feel confident in drawing six major conclusions:

⇨ The vast majority of farms in the world today are small and getting smaller

⇨ Small farms are currently squeezed onto less than a quarter of the world's farmland

⇨ We are fast losing farms and farmers in many places, while big farms are getting bigger

⇨ Small farms continue to be the major food producers in the world

⇨ Small farms are overall more productive than big farms

⇨ Most small farmers are women.

Many of these conclusions might seem obvious, but two things shocked us.

One was to see the extent of land concentration today, a problem that agrarian reform programmes of the 20th century were supposed to have solved. What we see happening in many countries right now is a kind of reverse agrarian reform, whether it's through corporate land grabbing in Africa, the recent agribusiness-driven coup d'état in Paraguay, the massive expansion of soybean plantations in Latin America, the opening up of Burma to foreign investors, or the extension of the European Union and its agricultural model eastward. In all of these processes, control over land is being usurped from small producers and their families, with elites and corporate powers pushing people onto smaller and smaller land holdings, or off the land entirely into camps or cities.

The other shock was to learn that, today, small farms have less than a quarter of the world's agricultural land – or less than a fifth if one excludes China and India from the calculation. Such farms are getting smaller all the time, and if this trend persists they might not be able to continue to feed the world.

28 May 2014

⇨ The above information is reprinted with kind permission from GRAIN. Please visit www.grain.org to read the report in full, or for further information.

Countries that have achieved the international hunger targets, by region				
Sub-Saharan Africa	Eastern, Southern and South-Eastern Asia, and Oceania	Latin America and the Caribbean	Caucasus and Central Asia	Northern Africa and Western Asia
Countries that met the MDG 1c target by halving the proportion of hungry people or bringing it under five per cent by 2015				
1. Benin	11. Bangladesh	22. Bolivia	27. Uzbekistan	28. Algeria
2. Ethiopia	12. Cambodia	23. Costa Rica		29. Iran
3. Gambia	13. Fiji	24. Mexico		30. Jordan
4. Malawi	14. Indonesia	25. Panama		31. Morocco
5. Mauritania	15. Kiribati	26. Suriname		
6. Mauritius	16. Lao People's Democratic Republic			
7. Mozambique	17. Malaysia			
8. Niger	18. Maldives			
9. Nigeria	19. Nepal			
10. Togo	20. Philippines			
	21. Solomon Islands			
Countries that maintained undernourishment below or close to five percent since 1990–92				
1. South Africa	2. Brunei Darussalam	4. Argentina	6. Kazakhstan	7. Egypt
	3. Republic of Korea	5. Barbados		8. Turkey
				9. Lebanon
				10. Saudi Arabia
				11. Tunisia
				12. United Arab Emirates

Source: The State of Food Insecurity in the World, Meeting the 2015 international hunger targets: taking stock of uneven progress, *Food and Agriculture Organization of the United Nations, 2015*

World footprint: do we fit on the planet?

Today humanity uses the equivalent of 1.5 planets to provide the resources we use and absorb our waste. This means it now takes the Earth one year and six months to regenerate what we use in a year.

Moderate UN scenarios suggest that if current population and consumption trends continue, by the 2030s, we will need the equivalent of two Earths to support us. And of course, we only have one.

Turning resources into waste faster than waste can be turned back into resources puts us in global ecological overshoot, depleting the very resources on which human life and biodiversity depend.

The result is collapsing fisheries, diminishing forest cover, depletion of freshwater systems, and the build up of carbon dioxide emissions, which creates problems like global climate change. These are just a few of the most noticeable effects of overshoot.

Overshoot also contributes to resource conflicts and wars, mass migrations, famine, disease and other human tragedies – and tends to have a disproportionate impact on the poor, who cannot buy their way out of the problem by getting resources from somewhere else.

Ending overshoot

The Earth provides all that we need to live and thrive. So what will it take for humanity to live within the means of one planet?

Individuals and institutions worldwide must begin to recognise ecological limits. We must begin to make ecological limits central to our decision-making and use human ingenuity to find new ways to live, within the Earth's bounds.

This means investing in technology and infrastructure that will allow us to operate in a resource-constrained world. It means taking individual action, and creating the public demand for businesses and policy makers to participate.

Using tools like the Ecological Footprint to manage our ecological assets is essential for humanity's survival and success. Knowing how much nature we have, how much we use, and who uses what is the first step, and will allow us to track our progress as we work toward our goal of sustainable, one-planet living.

Earth Overshoot Day 2015

In less than eight months, humanity has used up nature's budget for the entire year, with carbon sequestration making up more than half of the demand on nature, according to data from Global Footprint Network, an international sustainability think tank with offices in North America, Europe and Asia.

Global Footprint Network tracks humanity's demand on the planet (Ecological Footprint) against nature's ability to provide for this demand (biocapacity). Earth Overshoot Day marks the date when humanity's annual demand on nature exceeds what Earth can regenerate in that year. Earth Overshoot Day has moved from early October in 2000 to 13 August this year.[1]

The costs of this ecological overspending are becoming more evident by the day, in the form of deforestation, drought, freshwater scarcity, soil erosion, biodiversity loss and the build-up of carbon dioxide in the atmosphere. The latter will significantly amplify the former, if current climate models are correct. Consequently, government decision-makers who factor these growing constraints in their policy making will stand a significantly better chance to set their nation's long-term economic performance on a favourable track.

"Humanity's carbon footprint alone more than doubled since the early 1970s, which is when the world went into ecological overshoot. It remains the fastest growing component of the widening gap between the Ecological Footprint and the planet's biocapacity," said Mathis Wackernagel, president of Global Footprint Network and the co-creator of the Ecological Footprint resource accounting metric. "The global agreement to phase out fossil fuels that is being discussed around the world ahead of the Climate Summit in Paris would significantly help curb the Ecological Footprint's consistent growth and eventually shrink the Footprint."

The carbon footprint is inextricably linked to the other components of the Ecological Footprint – cropland, grazing land, forests and productive land built over with buildings and roads. All these demands compete for space. As more is being demanded for food and timber products, fewer productive areas are available to absorb carbon from fossil fuel. This means carbon emissions accumulate in the atmosphere rather than being fully absorbed.

A second chance

The climate agreement expected at the United Nations Conference of Parties (COP) 21 this December will focus on maintaining global warming within the two-degrees-Celsius range over pre-Industrial Revolution levels. This shared goal will require nations to implement policies to completely phase out fossil fuels by 2070, per the recommendations of the UN's Intergovernmental Panel on Climate Change (IPCC), directly impacting the Ecological Footprints of nations.

1 New data on China's coal consumption significantly alters our calculation, ultimately moving Earth Overshoot Day to August 9, four days earlier on the calendar.
This week China's statistical agency quietly published new data indicating China has been consuming up to 17% more coal a year than previously reported.
In 2012 alone, China consumed 600 metric tons more coal than previously indicated, which is equivalent to 70% of annual coal use in the United States, according to a New York Times article. This means China has released nearly one billion more tons of carbon dioxide a year than previous data shows – a massive upward revision.
China's revised coal numbers result in a 1.6% increase in humanity's Ecological Footprint, pulling Earth Overshoot Day four days earlier.
All official forecasts and emission policies were based on China's previous data. Global leaders will have to face these implications in the upcoming climate talks in Paris in December. The numbers suggest it may be more difficult for China to cap its carbon emissions by 2030, as pledged by President Xi Jingping, generating much optimism last year. Or perhaps the news will propel even more nations, cities, businesses and leaders to up the ante with their own climate change mitigation efforts.

Oops! Earth Overshoot Day 2015 was four days earlier, given China's revised carbon data

Earlier this year, Global Footprint Network calculated that Earth Overshoot Day landed on August 13. But new data on China's coal consumption significantly alters our calculation, ultimately moving Earth Overshoot Day to August 9, four days earlier on the calendar.

China's statistical agency quietly published new data indicating China has been consuming up to 17% more coal a year than previously reported. In 2012 alone, China consumed 600 metric tons more coal than previously indicated, which is equivalent to 70% of annual coal use in the United States, according to a New York Times article. This means China has released nearly one billion more tons of carbon dioxide a year than previous data shows – a massive upward revision.

China's revised coal numbers result in a 1.6% increase in humanity's Ecological Footprint, pulling Earth Overshoot Day four days earlier.

All official forecasts and emission policies were based on China's previous data. Global leaders will have to face these implications in the upcoming climate talks in Paris in December. The numbers suggest it may be more difficult for China to cap its carbon emissions by 2030, as pledged by President Xi Jingping, generating much optimism last year. Or perhaps the news will propel even more nations, cities, businesses and leaders to up the ante with their own climate change mitigation efforts.

Assuming global carbon emissions are reduced by at least 30 per cent below today's levels by 2030, in keeping with the IPCC's suggested scenario, Earth Overshoot Day could be moved back on the calendar to 16 September, 2030 (assuming the rest of the Footprint would continue to expand at the current rate), according to Global Footprint Network.

This is not impossible. In fact, Denmark has cut its emissions over the last two decades at this rate. Since the 1990s, it reduced its carbon emissions by 33 per cent. Had the world done the same (while not changing the rest of the Footprint), Earth Overshoot Day would be on 3 October this year.

This is not to say that Denmark has already reached a sustainable Ecological Footprint. Humanity would require the resources of nearly three planets if everyone lived like the Danes, which would move Earth Overshoot Day to 8 May.

Business as usual

By contrast, business as usual would mean using the resources equivalent to two planets by 2030, with Earth Overshoot Day moving up on the calendar to the end of June.

This projection assumes that biocapacity, population growth and consumption trends remain on their current trajectories. However, it is not clear whether a sustained level of overuse is possible without significantly damaging long-term biocapacity, with consequent impacts on consumption and population growth.

Tipping point

"We are encouraged by the recent developments on the front line of renewable energy, which have been accelerating worldwide, and by the increasing awareness of the finance industry that a low-carbon economy is the

way of the future," said Wackernagel. "Going forward, we cannot stress enough the vital importance of reducing the carbon footprint, as nations are slated to commit to in Paris. It is not just good for the world, but increasingly becoming an economic necessity for each nation. We all know that the climate depends on it, but that is not the full story: sustainability requires that everyone live well, within the means of one planet. This can only be achieved by keeping our Ecological Footprint within our planet's resource budget."

Additional resources:

⇨ More on Earth Overshoot Day: www.overshootday.org

⇨ Follow on social media: #overshoot

⇨ To calculate your own personal Ecological Footprint, and learn what you can do to reduce it, go to: www.footprintcalculator.org

⇨ Free Public Data Package (Ecological Footprint Data on 182 countries): www.footprintnetwork.org/public2015.

About Global Footprint Network:

Global Footprint Network is an international think tank working to drive informed, sustainable policy decisions in a world of limited resources. Together with its partners, Global Footprint Network coordinates research, develops methodological standards, and provides decision-makers with a menu of tools to help the human economy operate within Earth's ecological limits.

⇨ The above information is reprinted with kind permission from the Global Footprint Network. Please visit www.footprintnetwork.org for further information.

© Global Footprint Network 2015

What is sustainable development?

"Sustainable development is development that meets the needs of the present, without compromising the ability of future generations to meet their own needs."

The concept of sustainable development can be interpreted in many different ways, but at its core is an approach to development that looks to balance different, and often competing, needs against an awareness of the environmental, social and economic limitations we face as a society.

All too often, development is driven by one particular need, without fully considering the wider or future impacts. We are already seeing the damage this kind of approach can cause, from large-scale financial crises caused by irresponsible banking, to changes in global climate resulting from our dependence on fossil fuel-based energy sources. The longer we pursue unsustainable development, the more frequent and severe its consequences are likely to become, which is why we need to take action now.

So is it all just about the environment?

Living within our environmental limits is one of the central principles of sustainable development. One implication of not doing so is climate change.

But the focus of sustainable development is far broader than just the environment. It's also about ensuring a strong, healthy and just society. This means meeting the diverse needs of all people in existing and future communities, promoting personal wellbeing, social cohesion and inclusion, and creating equal opportunity.

If sustainable development focuses on the future, does that mean we lose out now?

Not necessarily. Sustainable development is about finding better ways of doing things, both for the future and the present. We might need to change the way we work and live now, but this doesn't mean our quality of life will be reduced.

A sustainable development approach can bring many benefits in the short to medium term, for example:

Savings – As a result of SDC scrutiny, government has saved over £60 million by improving efficiency across its estate.

Health and transport – Instead of driving, switching to walking or cycling for short journeys will save you money, improve your health and is often just as quick and convenient.

How does it affect me?

The way we approach development affects everyone. The impacts of our decisions as a society have very real consequences for people's lives. Poor planning of communities, for example, reduces the quality of life for the people who live in them. (Relying on imports rather than growing food locally puts the UK at risk of food shortages.)

Sustainable development provides an approach to making better decisions on the issues that affect all of our lives. By incorporating health plans into the planning of new communities, for instance, we can ensure that residents have easy access to healthcare and leisure facilities. (By encouraging more sustainable food supply chains, we can ensure the UK has enough food for the long-term future.)

⇨ The above information is reprinted with kind permission from the Sustainable Development Commission. Please visit www. sd-commission.org.uk for further information.

© Sustainable Development Commission 2015

How green is your city? Towards an index of urban sustainability

***An article from* The Conversation.**

THE CONVERSATION

By John Rennie Short, Professor, School of Public Policy, University of Maryland, Baltimore County

More than half of the world's population lives in cities and that percentage continues to rise, making cities critical areas for adopting practices to preserve natural resources.

How green is your city? How does it match up to other cities? Is it making progress in becoming more sustainable?

There is no definitive list but we may be moving toward clearer answers to these questions. An exciting body of work is coming up with ways to measure the environmental impact of cities. Let's look at three.

Land, energy, water

The ecological footprint measures how much land and water area a city requires to produce the resources it consumes and to absorb its wastes.

Ecological footprint is measured in global hectares (gha) per capita. The global average is around 2.6. The footprint of London UK, for example, was measured at 4.5, slightly lower than the UK average of 4.6. More people in London use public transport than almost any other city in the UK, reducing the relative size of its footprint.

When the data are broken down by neighbourhood, the biggest footprints are found in higher income areas where residents have larger homes and are more likely to have private automobiles. In San Francisco the value was calculated at 7.1 gha while in Calgary, Canada the value was 9.8 gha. Winters are cold in Calgary and most people use cars to get around.

Another measure is a city's carbon footprint, which is the total amount of greenhouse gases it produces. The basic unit is kg or ton of CO_2. The global average is 1.19 metric tons per person. One 2010 study measured the carbon footprint of 12 cities: Beijing, Jakarta, London, Los Angeles, Manila, Mexico City, New Delhi, New York, São Paulo, Seoul, Singapore and Tokyo. The number included direct emissions from the metropolitan area, as well as emissions produced in the metro area but consumed elsewhere, such as goods manufactured in cities.

Four of the cities have footprints smaller than the global average: Delhi, Manila, São Paulo and Beijing, in part because of relatively high usage of public transportation. London was close to the global average, while Los Angeles had by far the largest, followed by Singapore, New York and Mexico City.

Another study from 2009 measured the carbon footprint of the largest 100 metro areas in the US and found the higher-density metro areas had the smallest footprint. An even more recent study of all US households found that those in suburban areas had a much higher footprint than those in the larger cities.

The water footprint of a city is a measure of all the fresh water used to produce all the goods and services consumed in the city. This is a very difficult metric to compute because it includes the volume of fresh water consumed from surface water and ground water, the volume of rainwater consumed and the volume of fresh water used to dilute the pollutants created by the production of all goods and services for the city.

Studies that assessed the footprint of Milan, Italy and Lijiang City, China showed how the increasing footprint was straining those cities' water supplies.

Imperfect measures but a start

These metrics are still in the early stages of development. There are lots of problems, including assessing the leakage of impacts from outside the city's boundaries; the quality of data, which is too often imprecise and collected at different times for other purposes; and the lack of comparability between studies.

The work is more embryonic than definitive. For example, we have yet to agree upon standard protocols for the data used and methods employed.

While the three metrics have problems in estimation and calibration, they constitute a start. Even at this still rudimentary stage, they provide some startling findings. Notably, these initial studies show that larger cities have smaller carbon footprints than smaller cities. And higher density cities have lower carbon footprints.

As we transition into a more urban future, this is cause for some hope and could offer direction on effective city planning. Certain urban forms reduce the carbon footprint; these include more compact urban growth, more mass transit and greater use of cleaner, more sustainable energy supplies for buildings and transportation.

We need to refine these metrics, develop new ones and so create a standardized and easily understood index of city sustainability. Perhaps the protocols for developing a city sustainability index should be on the agenda at the United Nations Climate Change Conference to be held in Paris later this year.

With better data and a standard index, policies can be evaluated, targets set and institutions held to account. By comparing these metrics, planners and citizens can see how sustainability-related factors correlate to how livable cities are. And a robust city sustainability index would benchmark where we are now and provide a measure of progress in the future.

13 March 2015

⇨ Information reprinted with kind permission from *The Conversation*. Visit www.theconversation.com for further information.

Water for a Sustainable World

An extract from the 2015 UN water report.

Water is at the core of sustainable development. Water resources, and the range of services they provide, underpin poverty reduction, economic growth and environmental sustainability. From food and energy security to human and environmental health, water contributes to improvements in social well-being and inclusive growth, affecting the livelihoods of billions.

Vision 2050: Water in a sustainable world

In a sustainable world that is achievable in the near future, water and related resources are managed in support of human well-being and ecosystem integrity in a robust economy. Sufficient and safe water is made available to meet every person's basic needs, with healthy lifestyles and behaviours easily upheld through reliable and affordable water supply and sanitation services, in turn supported by equitably extended and efficiently managed infrastructure. Water resources management, infrastructure and service delivery are sustainably financed. Water is duly valued in all its forms, with wastewater treated as a resource that avails energy, nutrients and freshwater for reuse. Human settlements develop in harmony with the natural water cycle and the ecosystems that support it, with measures in place that reduce vulnerability and improve resilience to water-related disasters. Integrated approaches to water resources development, management and use – and to human rights – are the norm. Water is governed in a participatory way that draws on the full potential of women and men as professionals and citizens, guided by a number of able and knowledgeable organisations, within a just and transparent institutional framework.

The consequences of unsustainable growth

Unsustainable development pathways and governance failures have affected the quality and availability of water resources, compromising their capacity to generate social and economic benefits. Demand for fresh water is growing. Unless the balance between demand and finite supplies is restored, the world will face an increasingly severe global water deficit.

Global water demand is largely influenced by population growth, urbanisation, food and energy security policies, and macro-economic processes such as trade globalisation, changing diets and increasing consumption. By 2050, global water demand is projected to increase by 55%, mainly due to growing demands from manufacturing, thermal electricity generation and domestic use. Competing demands impose difficult allocation decisions and limit the expansion of sectors critical to sustainable development, in particular food production and energy. The competition for water – between water 'uses' and water 'users' – increases the risk of localised conflicts and continued inequities in access to services, with significant impacts on local economies and human well-being.

Over-abstraction is often the result of out-dated models of natural resource use and governance, where the use of resources for economic growth is under-regulated and undertaken without appropriate controls. Groundwater supplies are diminishing, with an estimated 20% of the world's aquifers currently over-exploited. Disruption of ecosystems through unabated urbanisation, inappropriate agricultural practices, deforestation and pollution are among the factors undermining the environment's capacity to provide ecosystem services, including clean water.

Persistent poverty, inequitable access to water supply and sanitation services, inadequate financing, and deficient information about the state of water resources, their use and management impose further constraints on water resources management and its ability to help achieve sustainable development objectives.

Water and the three dimensions of sustainable development

Progress in each of the three dimensions of sustainable development – social, economic and environmental – is bound by the limits imposed by finite and often vulnerable water resources and the way these resources are managed to provide services and benefits.

Poverty and social equity

While access to household water supplies is critical for a family's health and social dignity, access to water for productive uses such as agriculture and family-run businesses is vital to realise livelihood opportunities, generate income and contribute to economic productivity. Investing in improved water management and services can help reduce poverty and sustain economic growth. Poverty-oriented water interventions can make a difference for billions of poor people who receive very direct benefits from improved water and sanitation services through better health, reduced health costs, increased productivity and time savings.

Economic growth itself is not a guarantee for wider social progress. In most countries, there is a wide – and often widening – gap between rich and poor, and between those who can and cannot exploit new opportunities. Access to safe drinking water and sanitation is a human right, yet its limited realisation throughout the world often has disproportionate impacts on the poor and on women and children in particular.

Economic development

Water is an essential resource in the production of most types of goods and services including food, energy and manufacturing. Water supply (quantity and quality) at the place where the user needs it must be reliable and predictable to support financially sustainable investments in economic activities. Wise investment in both hard and soft infrastructure that is adequately financed, operated and maintained facilitates the structural changes necessary to foster advances in many productive areas of the economy. This often means more income opportunities to enhance expenditure in health and education, reinforcing a self-sustained dynamic of economic development.

Many benefits may be gained by promoting and facilitating use of the best available technologies and management systems in water provision, productivity and efficiency, and by improving water allocation mechanisms. These types of interventions and investments reconcile the continuous increase in water use with the need to preserve the critical environmental assets on which the provision of water and the economy depends.

Environmental protection and ecosystem services

Most economic models do not value the essential services provided by freshwater ecosystems, often leading to unsustainable use of water resources and ecosystem degradation. Pollution from untreated residential and industrial wastewater and agricultural run-off also weakens the capacity of ecosystem to provide water-related services.

Ecosystems across the world, particularly wetlands, are in decline. Ecosystem services remain under-valued, under-recognised and under-utilised within most current economic and resource management approaches. A more holistic focus on ecosystems for water and development that maintains a beneficial mix between built and natural infrastructure can ensure that benefits are maximised.

Economic arguments can make the preservation of ecosystems relevant to decision-makers and planners. Ecosystem valuation demonstrates that benefits far exceed costs of water-related investments in ecosystem conservation. Valuation is also important in assessing trade-offs in ecosystem conservation, and can be used to better inform development plans. Adoption of 'ecosystem-based management' is key to ensuring water long-term sustainability.

Published in 2015

Citation: WWAP (United Nations World Water Assessment Programme). 2015. The United Nations World Water Development Report 2015: Water for a Sustainable World. Paris, UNESCO.

⇨ The above information is reprinted with kind permission from UNESCO. Please visit en.unesco.org for further information.

> "In a sustainable world that is achievable in the near future, water and related resources are managed in support of human well-being and ecosystem integrity in a robust economy. Sufficient and safe water is made available to meet every person's basic needs, with healthy lifestyles and behaviours easily upheld through reliable and affordable water supply and sanitation services, in turn supported by equitably extended and efficiently managed infrastructure."

It's time to shout stop on this war on the living world

Our consumption is trashing a natural world infinitely more fascinating and intricate than the stuff we produce.

By George Monbiot

This is a moment at which anyone with the capacity for reflection should stop and wonder what we are doing.

If the news that in the past 40 years the world has lost over 50% of its vertebrate wildlife (mammals, birds, reptiles, amphibians and fish) fails to tell us that there is something wrong with the way we live, it's hard to imagine what could. Who believes that a social and economic system which has this effect is a healthy one? Who, contemplating this loss, could call it progress?

In fairness to the modern era, this is an extension of a trend that has lasted some two million years. The loss of much of the African megafauna – sabretooths and false sabretooths, giant hyaenas and amphicyonids (bear dogs), several species of elephant – coincided with the switch towards meat eating by hominims (ancestral humans). It's hard to see what else could have been responsible for the peculiar pattern of extinction then.

As we spread into other continents, their megafauna almost immediately collapsed. Perhaps the most reliable way of dating the first arrival of people anywhere is the sudden loss of large animals. The habitats we see as pristine – the Amazon rainforest or coral reefs for example – are in fact almost empty: they have lost

most of the great beasts that used to inhabit them, which drove crucial natural processes.

Since then we have worked our way down the foodchain, rubbing out smaller predators, medium-sized herbivores, and now, through both habitat destruction and hunting, wildlife across all classes and positions in the foodweb. There seems to be some kink in the human brain that prevents us from stopping, that drives us to carry on taking and competing and destroying, even when there is no need to do so.

But what we see now is something new: a speed of destruction that exceeds even that of the first settlement of the Americas, 14,000 years ago, when an entire hemisphere's ecology was transformed through a firestorm of extinction within a few dozen generations, in which the majority of large vertebrate species disappeared.

Many people blame this process on human population growth, and there's no doubt that it has been a factor. But two other trends have developed even faster and further. The first is the rise in consumption; the second is amplification by technology. Every year, new pesticides, fishing technologies, mining methods, techniques for processing trees are developed. We are waging an increasingly asymmetric war against the living world.

But why are we at war? In the rich nations, which commission much of this destruction through imports, most of our consumption has nothing to do with meeting human needs.

"One of the remarkable characteristics of recent growth in the rich world is how few people benefit"

This is what hits me harder than anything: the disproportion between what we lose and what we gain. Economic growth in a country whose primary and secondary needs have already been met means developing ever more useless stuff to meet ever fainter desires.

For example, a vague desire to amuse friends and colleagues (especially through the Secret Santa nonsense) commissions the consumption of thousands of tonnes of metal and plastic, often confected into complex electronic novelties: toys for adults. They might provoke a snigger or two, then they are dumped in a cupboard. After a few weeks, scarcely used, they find their way into landfill.

In a society bombarded by advertising and driven by the growth imperative, pleasure is reduced to hedonism and hedonism is reduced to consumption. We use consumption as a cure for boredom, to fill the void that an affectless, grasping, atomised culture creates, to brighten the grey world we have created.

We care ever less for the possessions we buy, and dispose of them ever more quickly. Yet the extraction of the raw materials required to produce them, the pollution commissioned in their manufacturing, the infrastructure and noise and burning of fuel needed to transport them are trashing a natural world infinitely more fascinating and intricate than the stuff we produce. The loss of wildlife is a loss of wonder and enchantment, of the magic with which the living world infects our lives.

Perhaps it is misleading to suggest that "we" are doing all this. It's being done not only by us but to us. One of the remarkable characteristics of recent growth in the rich world is how few people benefit. Almost all the gains go to a tiny number of people: one study suggests that the richest 1% in the United States capture 93% of the increase in incomes that growth delivers. Even with growth rates of 2% or 3% or more, working conditions for most people continue to deteriorate, as we find ourselves on short contracts, without full employment rights, without the security or the choice or the pensions their parents enjoyed.

"In the past 40 years the world has lost over 50% of its vertebrate wildlife (mammals, birds, reptiles, amphibians and fish)"

Working hours rise, wages stagnate or fall, tasks become duller, more stressful and harder to fulfil, emails and texts and endless demands clatter inside our heads, shutting down the ability to think, corners are cut, services deteriorate, housing becomes almost impossible to afford, there's ever less money for essential public services. What and whom is this growth for?

It's for the people who run or own the banks, the hedge funds, the mining companies, the advertising firms, the lobbying companies, the weapons manufacturers, the buy-to-let portfolios, the office blocks, the country estates, the offshore accounts. The rest of us are induced to regard it as necessary and desirable through a system of marketing and framing so intensive and all-pervasive that it amounts to brainwashing.

A system that makes us less happy, less secure, that narrows and impoverishes our lives, is presented as the only possible answer to our problems. There is no alternative – we must keep marching over the cliff. Anyone who challenges it is either ignored or excoriated.

And the beneficiaries? Well they are also the biggest consumers, using their spectacular wealth to exert impacts thousands of times greater than most people achieve. Much of the natural world is destroyed so that the very rich can fit their yachts with mahogany, eat bluefin tuna sushi, scatter ground rhino horn over their food, land their private jets on airfields carved from rare grasslands, burn in one day as much fossil fuel as the average global citizen uses in a year.

Thus the Great Global Polishing proceeds, wearing down the knap of the Earth, rubbing out all that is distinctive and peculiar, in human culture as well as nature, reducing us to replaceable automata within a homogenous global workforce, inexorably transforming the riches of the natural world into a featureless monoculture.

Is this not the point at which we shout stop? At which we use the extraordinary learning and expertise we have developed to change the way we organise ourselves, to contest and reverse the trends that have governed our relationship with the living planet for the past two million years, and that are now destroying its remaining features at astonishing speed?

Is this not the point at which we challenge the inevitability of endless growth on a finite planet? If not now, when?

1 October 2014

⇨ The above information is reprinted with kind permission from *The Guardian*. Please visit www.theguardian.com for further information.

Transforming our world: the 2030 Agenda for Sustainable Development

Preamble

This Agenda is a plan of action for people, planet and prosperity. It also seeks to strengthen universal peace in larger freedom. We recognise that eradicating poverty in all its forms and dimensions, including extreme poverty, is the greatest global challenge and an indispensable requirement for sustainable development. All countries and all stakeholders, acting in collaborative partnership, will implement this plan. We are resolved to free the human race from the tyranny of poverty and want and to heal and secure our planet. We are determined to take the bold and transformative steps which are urgently needed to shift the world onto a sustainable and resilient path. As we embark on this collective journey, we pledge that no one will be left behind. The 17 Sustainable Development Goals and 169 targets which we are announcing today demonstrate the scale and ambition of this new universal Agenda. They seek to build on the Millennium Development Goals and complete what these did not achieve. They seek to realise the human rights of all and to achieve gender equality and the empowerment of all women and girls. They are integrated and indivisible and balance the three dimensions of sustainable development: the economic, social and environmental.

The Goals and targets will stimulate action over the next 15 years in areas of critical importance for humanity and the planet:

People

We are determined to end poverty and hunger, in all their forms and dimensions, and to ensure that all human beings can fulfil their potential in dignity and equality and in a healthy environment.

Planet

We are determined to protect the planet from degradation, including through sustainable consumption and production, sustainably managing its natural resources and taking urgent action on climate change, so that it can support the needs of the present and future generations.

Prosperity

We are determined to ensure that all human beings can enjoy prosperous and fulfilling lives and that economic, social and technological progress occurs in harmony with nature.

Peace

We are determined to foster peaceful, just and inclusive societies which are free from fear and violence. There can be no sustainable development without peace and no peace without sustainable development.

Partnership

We are determined to mobilise the means required to implement this Agenda through a revitalised Global Partnership for Sustainable Development, based on a spirit of strengthened global solidarity, focused

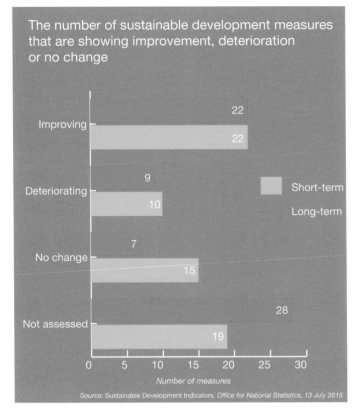

The number of sustainable development measures that are showing improvement, deterioration or no change

Improving: 22 (Short-term), 22 (Long-term)
Deteriorating: 9 (Short-term), 10 (Long-term)
No change: 7 (Short-term), 15 (Long-term)
Not assessed: 28 (Short-term), 19 (Long-term)

Number of measures

Source: Sustainable Development Indicators, Office for National Statistics, 13 July 2015

in particular on the needs of the poorest and most vulnerable and with the participation of all countries, all stakeholders and all people.

The interlinkages and integrated nature of the Sustainable Development Goals are of crucial importance in ensuring that the purpose of the new Agenda is realised. If we realise our ambitions across the full extent of the Agenda, the lives of all will be profoundly improved and our world will be transformed for the better.

Sustainable Development Goals

1. No poverty

End poverty in all its forms everywhere.

2. Zero hunger

End hunger, achieve food security and improved nutrition and promote sustainable agriculture.

3. Good health and wellbeing

Ensure healthy lives and promote wellbeing for all at all ages.

4. Quality education

Ensure inclusive and equitable quality education and promote lifelong learning opportunities for all.

5. Gender equality

Achieve gender equality and empower all women and girls.

6. Clean water and sanitation

Ensure availability and sustainable management of water and sanitation for all.

7. Affordable and clean energy

Ensure access to affordable, reliable, sustainable and modern energy for all.

8. Decent work and economic growth

Promote sustained, inclusive and sustainable economic growth, full and productive employment and decent work for all.

9. Industry, innovation and infrastructure

Build resilient infrastructure, promote inclusive and sustainable industrialisation and foster innovation.

10. Reduce inequalities

Reduce inequalities within and among countries.

11. Sustainable cities and communities

Make cities and human settlements inclusive, safe, resilient and sustainable.

12. Responsible consumption and production

Ensure sustainable consumption and production patterns.

13. Climate action

Take urgent action to combat climate change and its impacts.

14. Life below water

Conserve and sustainably use the oceans, seas and marine resources for sustainable development.

15. Life on land

Protect, restore and promote sustainable use of terrestrial ecosystems, sustainably manage forests, combat desertification, and halt and reverse land degradation and halt biodiversity loss.

16. Peace, justice and strong institutions

Promote peaceful and inclusive societies for sustainable development, provide access to justice for all and build effective, accountable and inclusive institutions at all levels.

17. Strengthen the means of implementation and revitalise the global partnership for sustainable development.

⇨ From *Transforming our world: the 2030 Agenda for Sustainable Development*, by the United Nations Department of Economic and Social Affairs

How much water is there in your boots?

Friends of the Earth has published major new research which sets out the environmental impact of making the products we use every day.

We want to live within the limits of what the planet can provide so first we need to measure what we are using. We asked environmental data experts Trucost to find out how much land and water is needed to make our food, our clothes and our gadgets – through the whole supply chain.

And it's a lot. A pair of leather boots could take 14 tonnes of water and $50m^2$ of land to make – mostly because of the massive resources used raising cattle. An extra ten tonnes of water is used if the leather tanning companies don't control their pollution though. Sadly that's common in places like Hazaribarch in Dhaka, Bangladesh.

By looking at the whole supply chain we were also able to discover the 'hotspots' – the processes that use up the most resources. For example, we found that 55% of the land needed to make a smartphone is actually used in the box it comes in, rather than the phone itself. Companies can use that information to cut down on waste.

Finally, we looked at companies as well as individual products. We found that Kraft Foods uses an area of land the size of Belgium and more than seven million Olympic-sized swimming pools of water to make chocolates.

We want companies to account for all the land, water, carbon and materials that are used in their whole supply chains, using the four footprints: land, water, carbon and materials.

It's good for companies and consumers too. We all need to be sure we've got a secure supply of the food and other products that we need to survive.

The new Government will have to take resources very seriously. Otherwise our environment and our economy will both suffer. That's why Friends of the Earth is calling on the new Government to carry out a review that we're calling a 'Stern for Resources'.

Four footprints

When we talk about the four footprints, we're referring to our land, water, material and carbon footprints.

Four footprints explained

To cut climate changing emissions we first measure how much we are emitting, then set targets to reduce them.

Why not do the same with consumption of resources?

One reason is that there is no agreement on how to measure the resources humanity uses. Which is where our work on resource use indicators, or 'footprints', comes in.

We've been working with Sustainable Europe Research Institute (SERI) in Vienna. They conclude that the best approach is to use four indicators which can apply to products, organisations or entire countries.

We're working to get the EU to adopt these four indicators as a way of measuring Europe's overall consumption – and then to set targets to reduce this resource use.

These indicators are:

i) Land footprint

The real land we are using for our food, timber and so on, wherever it is in the world. This can also be referred to as 'virtual land', 'embedded land' or 'global cropland'. We have set up a land footprint coalition calling for Europe to measure and reduce its land footprint.

ii) Water footprint

The quantity of water used in the life cycle of a product or by a country.

The Water Footprint Network has information on the water footprints of countries and products.

iii) Material footprint

The total tonnage of material extracted to make a product, or a country's consumption.

See our report *Overconsumption? Our use of the world's resources* for more information.

iv) Carbon footprint

The greenhouse gas emissions produced during the life cycle of a product. Or the emissions produced by a country, including from consumption of goods, wherever they happen in the world.

The UK Committee on Climate Change has published a detailed analysis of the UK's carbon footprint.

Further reading

Key briefing – The Four Footprints: increasing our resource efficiency, reducing our social and environmental impacts

2015

⇨ The above information is reprinted with kind permission from the Friends of the Earth Trust. Please visit www.foe.co.uk for further information.

How do we achieve a sustainable lifestyle?

By Rupert Blackstone, with contributions from Roger Middleton, Brian Robinson and Ian Arbon

Introduction

Although many of us, if not most of us, have some idea of what sustainability means conceptually, how many of us have an idea of what this means in terms of our lifestyle and personal responsibilities? Where the progress of society towards a sustainable future may be viewed as inadequate, it may be easy for us to blame governments and corporations, but given that the activities of governments and organisations serve individuals, what can we as individuals do and influence? How can engineers empower and equip us to live sustainably from day to day and what might a sustainable lifestyle look like? This is the first in a series of Energy, Environment and Sustainability Group (EESG) articles on what a sustainable lifestyle might mean in practice and what engineers can do to influence this. This is an extensive and complex subject that cannot be done justice in one article, but hopefully as we develop the theme there may be an exchange of ideas that can help us all move in the right direction.

Sustainability is generally understood to mean something along the lines of not consuming resources faster than their production and not polluting the environment in an irreversible way. These resources may be environmental, economic or indeed societal. Many people believe they are living sustainably because they are doing better than others around them by for example separating their rubbish for recycling more than others or riding a bicycle to work rather than driving. How do we know though if we are doing enough? Even those who work professionally in the area of sustainability rarely have truly sustainable lifestyles themselves, even if they advocate them for others. Often people suggest that they are not prepared to live sustainably as individuals until there is a collective movement with those around them doing the same; otherwise there is a feeling of self-sacrifice with little notable impact whilst those around them continue to live in relative luxury. Furthermore, responsibility is often transferred when it is said that we need the development of centralised systems before we can live a fully sustainable lifestyle. For example, it is often asked, "Why should we avoid using our car if the bus and railway systems are so inadequate?"

Approach towards understanding the practical consideration of sustainability in our lifestyles

For us to understand the potential both for sustainable engineering solutions and sustainable lifestyle choices, we may consider the sustainability of our lifestyles through subdivision into the following categories:

⇨ Energy including transport

⇨ Finite resource depletion and waste management

⇨ Water.

In fact there is much overlap between these categories, so the subdivision is not rigid. For example, water and energy can have opposing sustainability impacts – desalination uses an abundant water resource but uses much energy; and concentrating solar power (CSP) makes use of an abundant energy resource but may draw from limited water resources for cooling. Certain new designs of wind turbines, which generate energy from a sustainable resource, are dependent on a rare earth, neodymium, which apart from being a scarce resource has a significant environmental impact. There are more common elements that are in short supply such as lead (used for lead acid batteries) and copper (used for cabling and other electrical components), presenting significant challenges for the extensive introduction of electric vehicles, which receive widespread support for a sustainable transport future, as alluded to further on in the article.

Using these categories as guidance, we may consider what we as citizens can do to live sustainably in our everyday lives and also consider the role of engineers in developing systems to help us live more sustainably.

How are we living at the moment?

The resources we need to support our current lifestyles, if they are not finite, are generated over differing timescales. The rate of consumption of these resources by humans is related to population. We need therefore to consider our lifestyles in the context of an increasing population. It might be said that the lifestyles that many of us in the UK have at the moment might be reasonably sustainable if there were many fewer of us on Earth and the population were stable. In the UK there is often a sense of futility when people question what differences to the world changes in their own lifestyle will make when there are rapidly growing populations in other countries, for example, China and India. What is not always recognised is that the per capita the impact of these countries is far lower – for example on average in the UK we have an impact that is around three times as much as that which is sustainable for the global population (UNDP Human Development report). However, it should be noted that the energy consumption per capita of these countries is rising very rapidly. It should be recognised that much of the impact we associate with countries such as China is as a direct result of activities in the West. When we compare our national greenhouse gas emissions as a nation with those of other countries, the governmentally approved accounting mechanisms generally fail to take into account the emissions associated with our consumption of products that have been produced elsewhere, or of the emissions from shipping the goods around the world. When this is taken into account the picture for the UK looks less satisfactory.

How do we measure the impact?

Before we start considering what improvements we might make to our lifestyle, we need to have a means of measuring them. Not only do we need to know what to do, but we need to know how much to do. The problem is that sustainability refers to many different flows of material and energy so we need to find ways of navigating complexity. One commonly used method is life cycle assessment. Resource consumption and waste production and their associated impacts are modelled over the life cycle of a system or product. This has a significant scientific component in the determination of physical impacts, but then becomes somewhat subjective when the relative importance of the impacts is assessed. For example, which is more of a concern – respiratory disease from local pollution or flooding as a result of sea-level change? You might get a different answer from someone in London and someone in Dhaka. This illustrates the importance of gauging the social aspect of sustainability. Some people might be happy living in a high technology sprawling urban jungle surrounded by monocultural genetically modified crops, whereas others may prefer a world with humans living more in harmony with nature. Clearly we need somehow to balance the needs of the world's population, but perhaps the most important requirement is to empower people to make informed decisions. The range of data presented to us and the extent of conflicting information can be overwhelming, and it can be difficult to know what is best. The right answer is not always obvious. For example, what form of hand drying has the least life cycle environmental impact – disposable paper towels, washable towelling in a rotary dispenser or electric hand drying? (Answer: electric hand drying.) And are those biodegradable plastic shopping bags really a good idea when they require comparable amounts of energy for their manufacture as an ordinary plastic shopping bag, which can at least be partially converted back into usable energy or recycled? With time the truth should emerge from the cacophony of data as did that about the health impacts of smoking after the clouds of vested interests had been dispersed. With the large amount of data needing to be processed, life cycle assessment generally requires expensive software and a trained practitioner. We can wait for someone else then to come up with the answers, but is there anything we can do to work out our impact ourselves? David Mackay in his book, 'Sustainable Energy – Without the Hot Air' presents a straightforward approach of representing our individual impact in energy terms as kWh/person/day. Whilst this approach does not account for aspects such as finite resource depletion and water, we can achieve much with energy – for example, we can

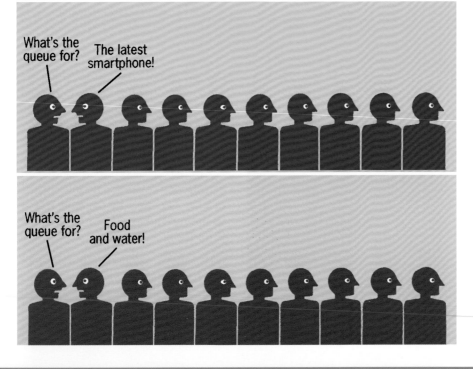

What's the queue for? The latest smartphone!

What's the queue for? Food and water!

make new materials or recycle old ones and desalinate water – so to express everything in terms of energy at least can give us some idea of our level of sustainability. Carbon dioxide may also be used as a measure of greenhouse gas emissions, an impact of general concern, and there are a number of 'carbon footprinting' tools available free on the web that can give some measurement of lifestyle impact. Carbon dioxide emission equivalent can be a useful way of expressing heat and electricity consumption in a common unit, although it should be recognised that as a measure of overall sustainability it is somewhat limited, and though there is a majority scientific view that human activity CO_2 emissions are having an impact on the climate, views on the degree and nature of the impacts are in flux.

Energy including transport

The energy required to support our lifestyle may be subdivided into the following categories:

⇨ Heating

⇨ Electricity for lighting and appliances

⇨ Transport

⇨ Embodied energy in products.

To all of these the energy hierarchy may be applied, which is broadly:

⇨ Avoid the use of energy

⇨ Use energy more efficiently

⇨ Renewable energy supply.

This can be expressed specifically for transport as the transport hierarchy, which may take the following form:

⇨ Avoid travel

⇨ Use efficient forms of transport

⇨ Use renewable forms of transport.

So what does this mean in practice?

Renewable energy is a constrained resource, given in particular the space required to convert it and also the intermittency of generation for most forms which make it challenging to align with demand.

Biomass allows control of timing of generation to supply a demand, unlike wind energy for example, but requires large areas of land as it is not a particularly efficient way of converting sunlight to energy, as compared to photovoltaics for example. Biomass can supply a proportion of current base load, but if we are to supply the rest of our demand from renewables we would largely be dependent on intermittent resources. Intermittency can to some extent be addressed through energy storage, but this is currently expensive. Increased interconnection between countries can also smooth intermittency. However, to a large extent the accommodation of intermittent renewable energy needs to come from demand management. Therefore, not only do we need to think about reducing our demand, but we also need to think about timing our consumption to coincide with availability of power. This can be done through a combination of occupier intervention and automated controls. The question is the extent to which people either want or feel able to time their energy consumption for optimum matching with renewable generation and how much should be automated. The best balance may be for people to have the option of making relatively simple choices, with more complex energy balancing being managed by control systems. This is an example of where there needs to be attention given to an effective interface between human behaviour and engineering solutions.

A large proportion of our energy consumption in the UK is for heating. Biomass heating can make a significant contribution, but with the constraints on biomass production, it is unlikely that this will meet all of our heating needs, in particular given the opportunities for heat consumption reduction in existing buildings are limited. Therefore, for renewable heating it seems likely that some form of electric heating will be required, through heat pumps for example. This gives the advantage of allowing extensive buffering of the intermittency of renewable energy

generation, giving the thermal inertia that is typical in heating buildings – building temperature does not generally change quickly if heating is switched off for a while, whereas for many electrical appliances such as televisions, the impact of a power dip can be significant. In terms of lifestyle choice, heating systems may be automated, but decisions need to be made as to the timing of heating and the temperature settings. In general we need to get used to far lower levels of heating and compensate by wearing more clothing indoors in winter, for example.

Conventional ways of powering transport cannot be easily sustained, for similar reasons as given for heating above. A switch from fossil transport fuels to biomass transport fuels is limited due to biomass being a constrained resource, and with current agricultural technology and availability of suitable land we would be unable to satisfy all our transport requirements through biomass. Therefore, it seems likely that there will be a need for electricity in some form to be used for transport. This may be used in conjunction with batteries or to synthesise a hydrocarbon or produce hydrogen for powering transport, but whichever way, transport presents an opportunity for the buffering of intermittency of renewable electricity generation.

Energy storage is a technology area for which there is room for much development. In general it is currently not economically viable apart from for niche circumstances, but with increasing volatility in energy prices and advancements in technology this is likely to change.

With the availability of feed-in tariffs (FiTs) and the Renewable Heat Incentive (RHI) to householders in the UK, there is increased interest in domestic generation, but is small-scale generation connected directly to a dwelling a good idea or is it better to focus on large-scale renewable energy generation? It is often suggested that building-integrated renewable energy generation is more efficient than remote large-scale generation for the reason that it does not suffer so much from distribution losses. However, this benefit is often outweighed by the increased efficiency of large-scale generation due to both the relationship between efficiency and scale and also the availability of more favourable resource remote from the built environment. It may be that for thermal generation, co-location of the generation with the building using the power allows the implementation of combined heat and power (CHP), using the waste heat from electricity generation to heat buildings. However an appropriate scale of CHP should be adopted to give an electrical efficiency that will allow the best use of fuel and satisfactory economic performance. This generally means not limiting the approach to energy generation on a single building, but serving a mix of buildings.

It is clear that with significant constraints on sustainable energy supply it is fundamental that attention is given to energy consumption reduction. Whilst much of this can be achieved through reduction of unnecessary consumption without a notable impact on quality of life, it is likely that some sacrifices will need to be made and getting people to accept this will be a major challenge. It is therefore critical that the societal dimension of sustainability is understood and delivered upon.

Finite resource depletion and waste management

In the same way that we may think in terms of an energy hierarchy and transport hierarchy, we may also consider the waste hierarchy. This may be expressed as:

⇨ Avoid generating waste

⇨ Re-use of waste

⇨ Recycle

⇨ Waste-to-energy

⇨ Landfill.

It is often thought that if we recycle our waste then we do not need to worry further about it. However, the energy use of recycling may be significant and indeed, in certain circumstances, actions three and four above may be interchangeable in that, in environmental terms, it may

be preferable to generate energy than recycle in considering the energy required for recycling. Increasingly thought is being given to treating waste as a resource rather than something to be disposed of. It is therefore helpful to think in terms of the life cycle of a material with more than one use. For example, wood may be used in construction with a view to it later being used as a fuel for energy generation. This is consistent with the emerging way of thinking referred to as the 'circular economy'. In the context of waste it can be demonstrated that whilst a zero-waste economy is thermodynamically impossible, there is much to be gained by focusing on product design and use, such that there can be a cyclic relationship between systems, thereby minimising waste – this may be a more helpful way of viewing waste management than the waste hierarchy.

So much of the production of our machines and materials depends on the extraction of substances from the Earth's crust that are not replenishable within the timescale of human existence. There is therefore a case for the increased production of materials from sustainable biological resources. An understanding of product life cycle is however critical since the production of biologically derived materials may require significant energy or even chemical input. For example, it may be that the production of cotton, with its use of fertilisers and pesticides might end up requiring more energy and polluting more than the production of certain artificial fibres.

Water

The availability of water suitable for drinking is of significant concern even in countries like the UK where flooding is not uncommon. Increasing population, associated food production and industrial processes are putting significant pressure on our water resources. As for energy and waste, the approach towards the sustainability of water may also be expressed as a hierarchy:

⇨ Avoid the use of water

⇨ Use water more efficiently

⇨ Renewable sourcing of water.

It is often thought that local supply of water, for example through rainwater harvesting on buildings, is preferable to large-scale water production. However, as for energy generation, it is often the case that centralised water treatment is more efficient than local water treatment even when taken into account distribution requirements.

In some parts of the world, such as Australia and China, there is extraction of fossil water reserves that cannot be replenished. Clearly, seawater is plentiful but desalination has a major energy penalty. However, it may be that desalination has a role to play in inter-seasonal energy buffering. Renewable energy resource generally not only varies diurnally, but also annually. Electricity storage is even a challenge economically when applied to buffering diurnal variations, but buffering of seasonal variations with electricity storage is currently untenable. Converting this energy to desalination of water and storage of potable water inter-seasonally may, however, be a worthwhile consideration for some locations.

Summary

With this article an attempt has been made to give an introduction to the various aspects that need to be thought through in moving towards a sustainable lifestyle. It is intended that subsequent articles will focus on specific aspects and explore practical considerations more fully. As individuals we need to consider what influence we can have over our own lifestyles and also influence those in government who implement systems that make this easier for us. For those of us who are engineers we need to consider what we can do to allow people to live more sustainably.

We all need to think globally and not just consider equations within our own ways of life.

2015

⇨ The above information is reprinted with kind permission from the Institute of Mechanical Engineers. Please visit www.imeche.org for further information.

Personal contribution to sustainability

The greatest long-term personal contribution that most people can make to sustainability is to refrain from having an unsustainable number of children, as explained in making the case for smaller families.

Nevertheless, the world is already very crowded and many resources on which we depend are becoming increasingly scarce. Although Population Matters' main focus is on the effect of human numbers, we also recognise the need to start reducing human impact on the environment as widely and as soon as possible. This means that those of us already enjoying high standards of living – the wealthy minority in developing countries and the majority of the population in the wealthier developed countries – need to take immediate action to reduce our 'footprint' on the planet.

The list below summarises a number of things that individuals can do. Some are simple and relatively painless, others are more difficult and require a greater level of commitment. The list is not intended to be exhaustive and many readers will be aware of more examples.

> **"The greatest long-term personal contribution that most people can make to sustainability is to refrain from having an unsustainable number of children"**

Travel and leisure

⇨ Plan journeys to use the most efficient means of travel and the optimum route

⇨ Walk or cycle rather than drive short journeys

⇨ Car share

⇨ Go by train or bus for medium/longer journeys (but note that empty buses or trains use more energy than a car, so provision of more public transport is not always the best long-term solution)

⇨ Holiday nearer to home, to reduce demand for air travel in particular

⇨ Work from home (even one day per week worked from home reduces the environmental impact of commuting by 20%)

⇨ Live nearer your workplace

⇨ Use a more economical car (but note that because a lot of resources and energy go into making cars, the lifecycle energy cost is not necessarily reduced by buying a new, more efficient car when an older one is still serviceable)

⇨ Drive more slowly (most cars are much more fuel efficient at 40–60mph than at 70mph)

⇨ Choose pastimes/hobbies that don't require large amounts of fuel, electricity or material resources

At home

⇨ Insulate the building to the best practicable standards (in the UK, high insulation standards for new buildings are specified in the building regulations but insulation of older buildings can often be improved. Sometimes this is prohibitively expensive, though upgrading loft insulation is usually cost-effective.)

⇨ Stop draughts, keep windows and doors closed during the heating season (but ensure sufficient ventilation to avoid condensation)

⇨ Turn off lights and appliances when not required

⇨ Use low-energy bulbs (high efficiency bulbs typically use less than 20% of the electricity for an equivalent light output compared to old-style (incandescent) bulbs)

⇨ Draw curtains or close shutters at night to reduce heat loss (daytime heat gain during hot weather can be minimised in a similar manner)

⇨ Set heating thermostats to the minimum comfortable temperature (similarly, set air conditioning to the highest comfortable temperature in hot weather)

⇨ Set heating system timers to operate only when the heat is required

⇨ Use natural ventilation rather than air conditioning whenever possible

⇨ Dress appropriately rather than heating the building more than necessary (note that in climates such as in the UK, a small reduction in heating temperature results in a proportionally large reduction in heat demand)

⇨ When cooking or making hot drinks, do not heat or boil more water than necessary

⇨ Avoid unnecessarily deep or frequent baths

⇨ Take showers as these generally use less water and heat than baths (but power showers have a high flow-rate and may use more water than a bath if run for more than five or ten minutes)

⇨ Use low water flush WCs

⇨ Use water efficient techniques for garden watering (plenty of tips can be found on the Internet)

⇨ Consider rainwater harvesting and grey water recycling

⇨ Use renewable energy (but check out the overall 'life cycle' energy costs of the equipment, supply and transport of renewable fuel, etc.)

⇨ Compost organic waste (check local regulations to avoid creating health hazards or other nuisances)

⇨ Explain the importance of sustainability to your family and friends

Goods and food

⇨ Reuse carrier bags and other containers rather than obtaining new ones

- Complain to retailers and manufacturers when goods are supplied with excessive amounts of packaging

- Insist that goods are properly labelled regarding origin, environmental standards, etc. (look for recognised and audited environmental assurance schemes; ask for carbon footprint information)

- Buy local wherever practicable (look for 'food miles' information – but note that buying seasonal food may be better than buying local food out of season if it is energy-intensive to grow)

- Adopt a lower meat content diet (there are environmental arguments for and against a vegetarian diet, but it is clear that a high meat content diet is less sustainable than a low meat one)

- Repair rather than replace items where possible

- When buying appliances that use water or energy, look for efficient models (but note that the environmental cost of manufacturing an item may outweigh any reduction in the environmental impact when in use; also some efficient devices may have so much energy 'embedded' in their manufacture that overall it may be better to use a simpler model)

- The above information is reprinted with kind permission from Population Matters. Please visit www.populationmatters. org for further information.

© Population Matters 2015

Grow your own; buy the rest from a wide range of outlets

The problem

We've lost touch with our roots

The UK was the first country in the world to industrialise so our families began to leave rural areas around 250 years ago to work in factories in towns and cities. Only around one in a 100 jobs are now on farms and, for most of us, neither our grandparents nor even great-grandparents were farmers. This means that most of us know very little about how our food is grown, what food is in season when, or even what fresh food – straight from the farm – tastes like. In 2010, yet another survey showed the extent of our ignorance by revealing that one in four children think the contents of a bacon sandwich come from a sheep! Cooking is not compulsory in all schools and in many homes parents are not able to teach their children to prepare healthy meals, either.

The power of the big supermarkets

Without first-hand experience of growing and cooking food, we often have to rely on what the food industry tells us – on the packaging and in ads – about the food we're buying. We're also buying food from fewer and fewer companies. In 2002 we bought half (50%) of our groceries from the four big supermarkets (Tesco, Sainsbury's, Asda and Morrisons) but this has now risen to around three-quarters (75%). In some ways this is understandable as supermarkets provide an apparently huge range of products at very affordable prices, all under one roof and at stores that are sometimes open 24 hours a day. But this concentration of market power in just a handful of companies can cause problems, for example:

The death of the high street and the rise of the 'clone town'

Most towns and high streets have now lost most of their independent butcher, baker and greengrocer shops. Supermarkets can often sell some staple products, such as factory loaves and milk, as 'loss leaders' – at a price below the costs of producing it, to attract customers into the store. They can make up the loss by passing the costs onto the suppliers (see below) or by charging more for other products in the store. Local specialist producers often cannot compete with this unfair pricing and are driven out of business.

Once local shops begin to close it can often spell the death of the high street, and means that our choice to shop there is lost. Those town centres that manage to hang on are now mostly dominated by chains, including smaller versions of the major supermarkets. A New Economics Foundation report describes these as 'clone towns', and shows the damage being done to the local area, including lost jobs and local identity.

Squeezing farmers out of business

In 2012, there were protests all over the country about the low price of milk in supermarkets forcing British dairy farmers out of business. Eventually agreement was reached to increase the price slightly, but it is not clear how long this agreement will last and this was just the latest example of farmers and other suppliers being treated unfairly by the major retailers. And it's not just British farmers that are under pressure. Poor farmers from poor countries are also squeezed by supermarkets' pressure for ever lower prices and for very stringent cosmetic standards for fresh produce.

This abuse of market power has led to a number of enquiries into the supermarkets' behaviour by the Competition Commission and to long-standing calls from a wide range of campaign groups for a supermarket ombudsman. This would have legal powers to make sure that, for example, supermarkets pay their suppliers promptly, have fair contracts that they can't pull out of at a moment's notice, and don't demand retrospective payments.

Campaign pressure has been successful, and the Government's Groceries Code Adjudicator (appointed in January 2013) will have legal powers, described by government as follows: "If the Adjudicator finds that retailers are breaching the Groceries Code and treating their suppliers unlawfully or unfairly, he or she will be able to apply a range of sanctions. In most cases, this would consist of recommendations or 'naming and shaming' but, if the breach is serious enough, the Adjudicator will have an immediate power to fine the retailer." However, the Adjudicator does not have a remit to tackle supermarkets on other ethical or environmental issues, nor on their promotion of junk food, including to children.

Putting all our eggs in four baskets

A smaller number of companies dominating the retail market has led to a smaller number of companies supplying them. Fewer and fewer companies are now able to supply the huge, year-round volume of products that supermarkets require. With fewer, but longer and more complex and inter-linked supply chains, the security risks rise. Contamination in just one part of the chain can mean the problem is spread across large parts of the whole food system, as the horsemeat scandal in 2013 so amply illustrated. Similarly, these supply chains rely on cheap oil, leaving us vulnerable to oil price rises, fuel protests or natural disasters. It has been suggested that this system, coupled with 'just in time' deliveries and low stock levels in stores means we are 'nine meals from anarchy'.

What we can do

Grow our own

Recent years have seen a resurgence in people wanting to grow their own food. In 2008, fruit and veg seed sales overtook flower seeds for the first time and in 2011 there were at least 87,000 people across the country on allotment waiting lists. In response to this demand, the Capital Growth campaign helped to create over 2,000 new community food growing spaces in London between 2008 and 2012. Similar initiatives are spreading to other towns and cities, supported by The Big Dig, and many areas also have Master Gardeners. All these groups, and many others, encourage people to use organic principles and practices in their growing activities. Among many other benefits, organic gardening reduces the risks to people and wildlife of using pesticides.

As well as growing more food and helping to 're-green' unloved patches of land, growing food in towns and cities can, as Garden Organic has noted: "...buffer the extremes of the urban environment – ameliorating temperatures, providing absorbent surfaces and preventing water run-off, filtering and cleaning air, not to mention absorbing carbon dioxide..

Community food growing can also bring communities together, provide skills that can improve employability, and enhance our health by reducing stress, increasing physical activity and encouraging us to eat more fresh and delicious produce.

Spread around our shopping pounds

The more money we spend with local outlets, the more it stays in our local area, helping to retain jobs and keep our town centres alive. It also means we're less likely to use our cars, and more likely to meet our neighbours on the stroll to or

from the shop or market – good for our health, keeping down the traffic, and for community spirit!

⇨ Find your local food enterprise at Big Barn

⇨ The Real Bread Campaign can help you find where to buy Real Bread locally

⇨ The Campaign for Real Ale runs a wide range of campaigns to help keep our local pubs open, as well as helping find and celebrate the ones that still are www.camra.org.uk

⇨ Farmers' markets continue to grow in popularity and the National Farmers' Retail and Markets Association can help you find one local to you, with London having its own farmers' market website

⇨ Street markets are promoted by the National Association of British Market Authorities

⇨ Food co-ops are another good way to get good quality food at an affordable price

⇨ You can find Community Supported Agriculture schemes here: www.soilassociation. org/communitysupported agriculture

⇨ agriculture/findacsa and there is also a wide range of box delivery schemes, providing local and often organic produce, up and down the country

⇨ Ethical Eats is Sustain's network for restaurants, caterers, community cafés and catering colleges that care about sustainability. The Ethical Eats team run regular workshops on sustainable food issues and help food businesses to identify more local and ethical suppliers. For more information see www.ethicaleats.org

⇨ The Sustainable Restaurant Association is a nationwide organisation that helps its members to operate in a more environmentally and socially sustainable way, and audits them on their performance. Look out for the SRA's 'Sustainability Champion'

badges in restaurant windows, or check out the directory of members on its website: www. thesra.org

Ask businesses and policy makers to take action

Local authorities can help the local food system to thrive by, for example:

⇨ Making land available for community food growing.

⇨ Adopting planning policies that encourage local food systems – read Sustain's 2011 report, *Good planning for good food*.

⇨ Supporting local food businesses – particularly those serving diverse and low-income communities with good food – community cafés, street markets, farmers' markets and other food outlets. This might be, for example, with business advice, reduced fees, parking and waste-collection arrangements, investing in 'destination shopping areas' featuring local food businesses to make them safer and more attractive, and promoting good, local food businesses with prominent signs and other marketing.

Stay informed

For general growing advice contact:

⇨ Garden Organic www. gardenorganic.org.uk

⇨ Good Gardeners Association www.goodgardeners.org.uk

⇨ Permaculture Association www. permaculture.org.uk.

To start or develop a community garden:

⇨ Community Land Advisory Service and Landshare can help you find land to grow on

⇨ The Federation of City Farms and Community Gardens has a wide range of information and advice

⇨ Garden Organic has a Master Gardener programme

⇨ The Women's Environment Network is the only organisation

working for women and the environment, and runs a number of community food growing projects

⇨ Sustain's Big Dig promotes food growing networks in UK towns and cities, particularly helping volunteers to find a local food growing space.

Want to go further and start generating some income with your food growing skills? Try these:

⇨ Growing Communities is a successful social enterprise and it also has a start up programme for communities wanting to set up profitable fruit and veg box schemes to support good food and farming.

⇨ The Wholesome Food Association promotes a "local symbol" scheme to encourage natural and authentic food and farming, educate about the health and social benefits of eating wholesome food, and help renew local economies and communities.

⇨ World Wide Opportunities on Organic Farms teaches people about organic growing and low-impact lifestyles through hands-on experience.

⇨ *A Growing Trade* is a guide for community groups growing food to sell in our towns and cities.

⇨ The above information is reprinted with kind permission from Sustain. Please visit www. sustainweb.org for further information.

£160-million technology boost for UK agricultural industries

The UK will become a world leader in agricultural science and technology following the launch of a new strategy.

The UK will become a world leader in agricultural science and technology following the launch of a new strategy to deliver sustainable, healthy and affordable food for future generations.

Breakthroughs in nutrition, informatics, satellite imaging, remote sensing, meteorology and precision farming mean the agriculture sector is one of the world's fastest growing sectors.

Developed in partnership with industry, the Agricultural Technologies Strategy will ensure everyone from farmers and retailers, to cooks and shoppers share the benefits these exciting opportunities bring.

It includes a £160-million government investment in developing cutting edge technologies, and taking innovative products such as cancer-fighting broccoli from the field to the shopping aisle.

Industry is also expected to invest heavily in the strategy which will transform farming in the UK, using the latest technologies to ensure the process is as productive as possible whilst reducing environmental impact and resource use.

With the demand for food rising rapidly worldwide, the strategy also aims to make the UK a world leader in addressing global food security issues.

Agri-tech is a well-established and important UK sector. The entire agri-food supply chain, from agriculture to final retailing and catering, is estimated to contribute £96 billion to the economy and employ 3.8 million people.

Universities and Science Minister David Willetts said:

"Some of the biggest brands in farming and food are based in the UK. We have a world-class science and research community and our institutes and universities are at the forefront of agricultural research.

"To get ahead in the global race, this strategy sets out how we can ensure that we turn our world-beating agricultural science and research into world-beating products and services."

This Agricultural Technologies Strategy follows the recent plans for automotive, construction, aerospace and other key sectors to secure sustainable future growth in the economy.

Defra Minister for Science Lord de Mauley said:

"We face a global challenge to feed the rapidly increasing population in a way which is affordable and sustainable.

"We are investing in technologies that will enable British farmers to meet these challenges and take advantage of the growing demand in export markets for British food."

To take advantage of agriculture's opportunities and drive growth the Agricultural Technologies Strategy sets out a range of key actions, including:

⇨ a £90-million government investment in world-class Centres for Agricultural Innovation with additional investment from industry. The centres will support the wide-scale adoption of innovation and technology across key sectors, technologies and skills in the food and farming supply chain. This includes up to £10 million for a Centre for Agricultural Informatics and Metrics of Sustainability which will use data from farms, laboratories and retailers to drive innovation

⇨ creating a £70 million Agri-Tech Catalyst to help new agricultural technologies bridge the so-called 'valley of death' between the lab and the marketplace. Co-funded with industry, the catalyst will specifically support small- and medium-sized enterprises. The investment includes £10 million to support the transfer of technology and new products to developing countries

⇨ the creation of an industry Leadership Council to unify the agriculture technology sector and make the UK more internationally competitive

⇨ the recruitment of a new UKTI agri-tech team to boost exports and overseas investment in the UK's agricultural technologies.

In addition also announced today:

⇨ £30 million for four agri-science research and innovation campuses by Biotechnolocy and Biological Sciences Research Council

⇨ a multi-million-pound scientific research partnership between Rothamsted and Syngenta to increase wheat productivity

⇨ The new Leadership Council will bring together representatives from the diverse agriculture sector, including food and farming production, industry, science and research, and government.

Judith Batchelar, Director of Sainsbury's brand, said:

"Farming is one of the biggest industries in the UK, which is why we think it's so important to plan for the future now.

"This is the reason I'm extremely proud to launch a graduate scheme today that's dedicated to British agriculture, it also adds to the 80 graduate placements we've offered in just the last five years. With the average age of a farmer being over 50 it's important to attract and train young talent to drive technical development in a sustainable way and build on Sainsbury's heritage in food technology and product development. The strategy and our scheme bring benefits for the whole supply chain – from farmers through to our customers."

As well as making sure basic research is turned into new products fit for the global market, the Leadership Council will work to change the way jobs in agriculture are perceived, making it an aspirational area of work that attracts and retains talented people.

International Development Secretary Justine Greening said:

"We promised at the Nutrition for Growth summit last month to put science at the heart of ensuring better nutrition for children in the developing world. The agri-tech strategy will help to deliver on that promise.

"British expertise is already changing lives. Supporting agriculture and food systems that address global malnutrition will help millions in Africa to lift themselves out of poverty for good."

22 July 2013

⇨ The above information is reprinted with kind permission from the Department for Business, Innovation & Skills, Department for Environment, Food & Rural Affairs, Lord de Mauley TD and The Rt Hon. David Willetts. Please visit www.gov.uk for further information.

Vertical farms offer a bright future for hungry cities

THE CONVERSATION

***An article from* The Conversation.**

By Tim Heath, Chair of Architecture and Urban Design, Faculty of Engineering, University of Nottingham and Yiming Shao, PhD candidate, University of Nottingham

The 21st century has seen rapid urbanisation and the global population is now expected to grow to more than 8.3 billion by 2050. Currently, 800 million hectares – 38% of the Earth's land surface – is farmed and we'll soon need to give over another 100 million hectares if we continue to use current agricultural methods. That's not additional fertile land that actually exists though, so some are investigating the potential of vertical farming.

It has been suggested that a 30 storey 27,800,000m² vertical farm could be achieved within one New York City block. That farm could feed 50,000 people, providing 2,000 calories for every person each day. With results like that as a prospect, it's easy to see why enthusiasts see vertical farms as the future.

Growing up

Vertical farms are still very much at the conceptual stage. The idea is to cultivate crops on multiple levels within high-rise buildings in urban areas. It's not an entirely new proposition, with architect Ken Yeang suggesting a vision of high-rise plant cultivation in mixed-use skyscrapers as early as the 1980s. Professor Dickson Despommier, the leading international advocate of vertical farms, describes them as "a global solution" to the world's urban food needs.

Vertical farms do indeed have many advantages. They would enable us to produce crops all year round using 70% less water. We wouldn't need to use agro-chemicals and could avoid the adverse environmental factors that affect yield and quality in more traditional farming. And if food were grown in urban areas in the first place, we could eliminate the financial and

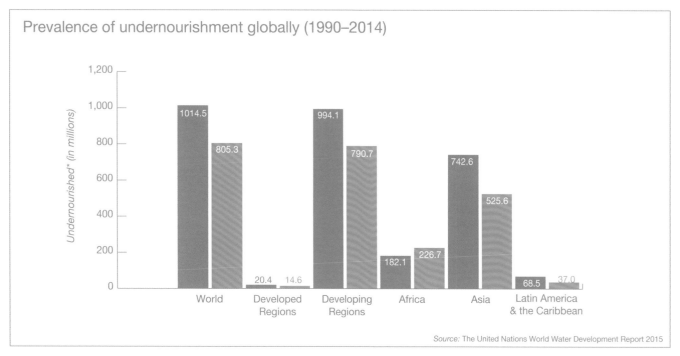

Prevalence of undernourishment globally (1990–2014)

Undernourished* (in millions)

World: 1014.5, 805.3
Developed Regions: 20.4, 14.6
Developing Regions: 994.1, 790.7
Africa: 182.1, 226.7
Asia: 742.6, 525.6
Latin America & the Caribbean: 68.5, 37.0

Source: The United Nations World Water Development Report 2015

environmental costs of importing food into towns and cities.

Growing pains

In some respects, farming is now a practical possibility. The technology it requires, in terms of plant growth and construction, are available. We can already cultivate plants without soil and recycle the water used to deliver clean indoor farming, for example. Hydroponics, where plant roots are grown in nutrients dissolved in water, is one option. This plant-growing technique can be combined with traditional aquaculture to raise fish or prawns – a farming technique known as aquaponics. Another way to grow plants is aeroponics, which involves growing suspended plants by spraying the roots with a nutrient-rich water solution.

But even though it has been more than 20 years since the concept was first proposed and the pressure of climate change continues to mount, vertical farming is still not a reality. The two biggest problems have been financial and technological viability, particularly when it comes to actually building these high-rise spaces.

Vertical farms need contemporary building materials and renewable energy systems. Sunlight reflecting and collecting devices such as light shelves, light pipes and fibre optics can deliver natural light deep into buildings to provide energy for photosynthesis.

The development of LED makes it possible for a vertical farm to operate without the need for sunlight but the cost and energy consumption are currently prohibitive. The initial cost could easily be more than $100 million for a 60-hectare vertical farm, which makes it unrealistic at the moment. But this could change as the price should drop rapidly as the technology develops. The obvious solution is to integrate natural light where conditions are suitable and LED in other parts of the building.

In the meantime, investors are likely to stay away. Vertical farms integrate advanced technologies and need to be relatively large-scale if they are to yield attractive results. It has been estimated that the return on investment for a 10-storey vertical farm would be approximately 8%, whereas investors typically seek a minimum rate of return of 10–12%. And since there are risks involved in developing a new type of building, investors are realistically more likely to want an annual return of around 15%. Again though, economic viability will undoubtedly come with technological improvements.

Making it happen

Progress is being made towards resolving all these issues so the next step will really be to get a prototype vertical farm up and running in an urban location. What few small-scale prototypes exist in the world are based mainly in research institutions. To be sure that the technique can work, we'll need to construct a high-rise structure in a more realistic environment. If it works, it could spark follow-up projects.

To make vertical farming a reality, we need the support of governments and pioneering organisations willing to take a punt. If they do, we could make a huge contribution to food security and could transform the everyday lives of city dwellers across the world. There are more than 26 cities with a population of over ten million, each requiring up to 7,000 tons of food to be imported to feed their residents – vertical farms could, be one of a package of more sustainable alternatives to feeding them.

21 July 2014

⇨ The above information is reprinted with kind permission from *The Conversation*. Please visit www.theconversation.com for further information.

© 2010-2015, The Conversation Trust (UK)

Eight ways business is helping to protect the environment

By Jade Rickman, Policy Adviser, CBI

The world is facing a number of environmental challenges; from global warming to resource efficiency and the UK has long been at the forefront of the effort to tackle these issues. Business understands its environmental impact and is taking action to be part of the solution creating a greener, low-carbon and more sustainable economy. Businesses are:

1. Putting environmental issues front and centre

Sustainability is no longer on the side-line in commercial planning but integral to operations, allowing businesses to reduce costs, enter new markets and improve corporate reputation. It affects everyone in a business from the CEO to those on the factory floor. Companies are looking at ways to cut waste, reduce energy usage or source raw materials sustainably. Many businesses going even further in their commitments, for example by reusing all waste or backing a global price on carbon.

2. Encouraging their global supply chains to do the same

For most businesses, sustainability plans now extend beyond their daily operations and into the entire supply chain. To determine its true environmental footprint, Nike looks at everything from raw materials production to how consumers dispose of products after use to measure and minimise its environmental impact.

3. Setting ambitious targets to cut their carbon emissions

All businesses use energy, and, manufacturing processes such as melting steel or firing bricks use a significant amount with the average yearly energy bill for a large industrial user costing almost £10 million. To mitigate this, many businesses are committed to cutting energy use and setting ambitious targets to reduce their carbon footprint. For instance, the cement sector is aiming for an 81% reduction in carbon emissions by 2050.

4. Building greener homes

Businesses are not only cutting their own carbon emissions but are creating the plans and products to build zero-carbon homes. Homebuilders are using sustainable materials and innovative products to construct homes that have zero – or even negative – carbon emissions. Using cutting-edge energy efficiency measures and harnessing renewable energy, the UK's housing stock is becoming ever greener.

5. Helping schools, hospitals and public buildings to reduce carbon

Sharing knowledge, skills and resources, business is helping to make our public buildings greener. Whether this is by educating children on global warming or providing solar panels for schools, programmes like British Gas' 'Generation Green' which helps over 13,000 schools across the UK by providing classroom resources, education experiences and sustainable energy technologies, go some way towards protecting the environment for future generations.

6. Making the things we buy more environmentally friendly and cheaper

From Toyota's Prius to Nissan's Leaf to Tesla's Model S, car manufacturers are competing to produce ever more fuel efficient, environmentally friendly models without comprising range, comfort and style. Not only are ours cars becoming more environmentally friendly, electrical manufacturers are working to make the electrical products we use more energy efficient and cheaper to run, which is good for the customer and good for the environment. For example, an energy saving fridge freezer could save up to £45 per year on energy bills.

7. Saving trees by planting rainforests and reducing paper waste

To halt deforestation and protect the rainforests of the world, businesses are putting back what they take out and being smarter with their paper usage. Since 2004, Sainsbury's has planted 2.2 million trees, the equivalent of four Sherwood Forests. Companies are monitoring closely their waste paper and recycling as much as possible.

8. Innovating to provide low-carbon solutions

Business isn't taking a back seat in the transition to a low-carbon economy but innovating to give the UK a leading edge in tackling climate change by developing technologies such as carbon capture and storage (CCS), hydrogen power or demand response. The UK has established itself an attractive place to invest in developing CCS, which is the only way to reduce emissions and keep coal and gas in the UK's long-term energy mix.

20 January 2015

⇨ The above information is reprinted with kind permission from The Great Business Debate. Please visit www.greatbusinessdebate.co.uk for further information.

Crowd votes with its feet to back tech firm that turns footsteps into electricity

Pavegen, the British kinetic energy pioneer, raises half its £750,000 crowdfunding round in the first day.

By Rebecca Burn-Callander

Pavegen, the British technology company that turns footsteps into energy, secured almost half of its £750,000 crowdfunding round on Tuesday within 12 hours of launching its campaign on the Crowdcube platform.

The kinetic energy pioneer has raised £334,000 from 138 investors with 40 days still to go. The company is offering an equity stake of just under 5% to "the crowd".

Founded in 2009, Pavegen has developed a patented flooring product that can be used indoors or outdoors in high traffic areas, and generates electricity from pedestrian footfall using an electromagnetic induction process. The company has now completed its 130th installation.

It exports its energy-converting tiles to 30 countries across the world. Customers range from infrastructure giants such as Siemens to retail brands Nike and Uniqlo. Pavegen is about to install its products outside the White House in Washington DC.

According to founder Laurence Kemball-Cook, interest in the campaign was driven by the company's latest installation in the City of London, which proved a hit with local bankers. Pavegen's technology was implemented by the Canary Wharf Group on Monday to power streetlights in the area.

"Testing the market there has been interesting," said Mr Kemball-Cook, who revealed that people working at nearby JP Morgan, HSBC and Barclays had invested in the crowdfunding round.

"People will pay the same amount as they would using a normal [energy] provider, except that we will power buildings and give them data about where people are walking"

"People are requesting a business plan every five minutes."

The fresh cash will be invested into bringing down the cost of Pavegen's tiles.

"We want to make our flooring products the same price as normal tiles," said Mr Kemball-Cook.

"When anyone wants to do the floor of an office, or a driveway, or when a council is paving the street, they will be able to pay the same amount as they would using a normal provider, except that we will power buildings and give them data about where people are walking."

This aim "cannot be achieved overnight", he added.

Company revenue to date is £2.5 million, and sales were up 20% in the second quarter of the year, compared to the first three months.

The company's new armchair investors on Crowdcube will be able to cash in their shares when Pavegen lists on the stock exchange or is acquired by another business.

"I see this as a mini IPO," said Mr Kemball-Cook. "The public is empowered by walking on our tiles, and now the same people are empowering us."

26 May 2015

⇨ The above information is reprinted with kind permission from _The Telegraph_. Please visit www.telegraph.co.uk for further information.

Pavegen introduces pedestrian power in UK's most sustainable building!

Pavegen and Siemens collaborate once more, taking people-power to the Crystal in London!

Pavegen has installed 11 tiles in the heart of the Crystal in Royal Victoria Dock, powering a LED bar that activates coloured lighting in response to visitor's footsteps. The footfall can also be used to track real-time data; calculating daily footfall levels as well as footsteps per tile. The installation allows Pavegen to demonstrate the potential of footfall energy in a public space; uniting communities through positive energy generation.

The project, in collaboration with global technology company Siemens, is 'catalytic' in setting standards for the future. The Crystal building is one of the world's most sustainable events venues, also offering office space for Siemens' Global Centre of Competence in Cities; emphasising their strategic focus on low-carbon, urban infrastructure solutions fit for the future.

Pavegen is a clean-technology company that generates electricity from footsteps. The innovative tiling solution converts the weight of a step into a continuous power source, using the electricity to power lighting, advertising and wayfinding signage.

The previous partnership with Siemens entailed installing tiles in the heart of Federation Square, Melbourne, Australia. This was one of Pavegen's first installations in the Asia Pacific region; a key market for

sustainability and clean-technology innovations. The tiles powered lighting in the area, raising awareness to the power of a footstep in smart cities. Since opening in 2002, Federation Square has seen over 100 million visits, and aims to become carbon neutral could establish Melbourne's vision of becoming a sustainable smart city of the future.

"With Siemens, we know we can prove that sustainability in the urban space is viable," Pavegen CEO and founder Laurence Kemball-Cook explained. "It's a huge step towards Pavegen's final goals in becoming a commercially viable energy solution."

Situated in East London, at Royal Victoria Dock, the Crystal is the first building to achieve the highest sustainable building accolade from both BREEAM (outstanding) and LEED (platinum). Aiming to make sustainability engaging and appealing, the establishment also contains a permanent exhibition on sustainable development, where Pavegen will take centre stage.

"As the world's largest exhibition focused on sustainable cities, we are constantly looking for exciting new technologies which can play an important role in the future of our cities. The Pavegen tiles form part of our new Kinetic Energy zone which will provide

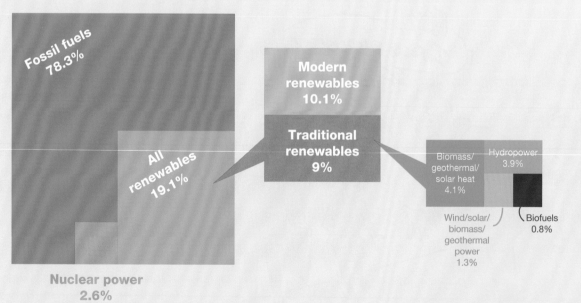

Estimated renewable energy share of global final energy consumption, 2013

Fossil fuels 78.3%

All renewables 19.1%

Modern renewables 10.1%

Traditional renewables 9%

Biomass/geothermal/solar heat 4.1%

Hydropower 3.9%

Wind/solar/biomass/geothermal power 1.3%

Biofuels 0.8%

Nuclear power 2.6%

i An estimated 1.2 billion people worldwide lack access to electricity, and 2.8 billion people rely on traditional biomass for cooking and heating. See United Nations Sustainable Energy for All (SE4ALL), "United Nations Decade of Sustainable Energy for All 2014-2024," http://www.se4all.org/decade/, viewed 10 April 2015.
ii - SE4ALL has three interlinked objectives: ensuring universal access to modern energy services, doubling the global rate of improvement in energy efficiency, and doubling the share of renewable energy in the global energy mix. See SE4ALL, "Our Objectives," http://www.se4all.org/our-vision/our-objectives/, viewed 10 April 2015.

Source: Renewables 2015, global status report, Renewable Energy Policy Network for the 21st Century. See Section 1, Endnote 9 for detailed information about sources of data.

an informative and fun experience for all visitors to the Crystal exhibition", says Josh Palmer, Operations Manager, The Crystal. Having recently welcomed its 250,000th visitor since opening in September 2012, the Crystal exhibition is looking to the future with over 15 new exhibits added in the last year.

About Pavegen:

Pavegen is the invention of Laurence Kemball-Cook, 29, an industrial design engineer and graduate of Loughborough University. The CEO and founder of Pavegen developed the concept in 2009, whilst researching kinetic off-grid energy solutions in environments where low-carbon technologies like solar and wind are not practical. Pavegen tiles can be used in both indoor and outdoor locations and work best where there is high footfall such as retail and transport hubs. The technology is integrated, discreetly, into the existing environment, underfoot. Permanent installations include three schools in the UK, the entrance of a large office and an installation at Federation Square, Melbourne – to name a few. Pavegen units are also available in modular form for use at events, such as exhibitions and marketing campaigns, to demonstrate their commitment to innovation, sustainability and CSR initiatives.

About the Crystal:

The Crystal is home to the world's largest exhibition focusing on urban sustainability and an award winning cafe. Located in Royal Victoria Dock, adjacent to the Emirates Cable Car, the Crystal is open from 10:00 until 17:00 Tuesday to Sunday. For more information: www.thecrystal.org

About Siemens AG:

Siemens AG (Berlin and Munich) is a global technology powerhouse that has stood for engineering excellence, innovation, quality, reliability and internationality for more than 165 years. The company is active in more than 200 countries, focusing on the areas of electrification, automation and digitalisation. One of the world's largest producers of energy-efficient, resource-saving technologies, Siemens is No. 1 in offshore wind turbine construction, a leading supplier of gas and steam turbines for power generation, a major provider of power transmission solutions and a pioneer in infrastructure solutions as well as automation, drive and software solutions for industry. The company is also a leading provider of medical imaging equipment – such as computed tomography and magnetic resonance imaging systems – and a leader in laboratory diagnostics as well as clinical IT. In fiscal 2014, which ended on 30 September, 2014, Siemens generated revenue from continuing operations of €71.9 billion and net income of €5.5 billion. At the end of September 2014, the company had around 343,000 employees worldwide on a continuing basis. Further information is available on the Internet at www.siemens.com.

30 October 2015

⇨ The above information is reprinted with kind permission from Pavegen. Please visit www. pavegen.com for further information.

Key facts

⇨ As a minimum a sustainable society, i.e. one that could physically be sustained indefinitely, would need a stable or reducing population, very high levels of reuse and recycling, 100% renewable energy and no net loss of soil and biodiversity. No country is yet near it. (page 1)

⇨ The resources we use and our impact on the environment effectively depend on three main factors:

  • Population – how many of us there are consuming and creating waste

  • Affluence, or consumption – the amount of goods and services on average we each use

  • Technology – how inefficiently/ harmfully we produce these goods and services (page 1)

⇨ Biodiversity is declining sharply, while our demands on nature are unsustainable and increasing. Species populations worldwide have declined 52 per cent since 1970. We need 1.5 Earths to meet the demands we currently make on nature. (page 2)

⇨ In less than two human generations, population sizes of vertebrate species have dropped by half. (page 2)

⇨ Humans are "eating away at our own life support systems" at a rate unseen in the past 10,000 years by degrading land and freshwater systems, emitting greenhouse gases and releasing vast amounts of agricultural chemicals into the environment, new research has found. (page 4)

⇨ The UK could run out of land to meet its growing demands for food, housing, green energy and environmental protection by 2030, according to a Cambridge University-backed report. (page 5)

⇨ A Defra spokesperson said: "We have good food security in the UK thanks to our own thriving £97.1 billion food and farming industry and trade access to markets across the globe. We are investing £70 million in agricultural technologies that will help us to increase the efficiency of food production and help our food, farming and science industries grow economically while meeting the increasing global demand for food." (page 5)

⇨ Each year, humans reduce the number of trees worldwide by 15 billion. (page 6)

⇨ Water demand has increased dramatically over the past quarter of a century, and we now use half as much water again as we did in 1980. (page 8)

⇨ For the first time in 20 years, the eatwell plate has been given a makeover. The World Wildlife Fund have proposed a Livewell 2020 Diet, which sees an increase in vegetable consumption by two per cent and a decrease in 'non-dairy protein' to balance the plate. (page 10)

⇨ Small farms occupy 60% of all arable land worldwide. (page 12)

⇨ More than half of the world's population lives in cities and that percentage continues to rise, making cities critical areas for adopting practices to preserve natural resources. (page 17)

⇨ Ecological footprint is measured in global hectares (gha) per capita. The global average is around 2.6. The footprint of London UK, for example, was measured at 4.5, slightly lower than the UK average of 4.6. More people in London use public transport than almost any other city in the UK, reducing the relative size of its footprint. (page 17)

⇨ In the past 40 years the world has lost over 50% of its vertebrate wildlife (mammals, birds, reptiles, amphibians and fish). (page 21)

⇨ A pair of leather boots could take 14 tonnes of water and 50m2 of land to make – mostly because of the massive resources used raising cattle. (page 24)

⇨ The UK was the first country in the world to industrialise so our families began to leave rural areas around 250 years ago to work in factories in towns and cities. Only around one in a 100 jobs are now on farms and, for most of us, neither our grandparents nor even great-grandparents were farmers. (page 30)

⇨ Recent years have seen a resurgence in people wanting to grow their own food. In 2008, fruit and veg seed sales overtook flower seeds for the first time and in 2011 there were at least 87,000 people across the country on allotment waiting lists. (page 31)

⇨ The 21st century has seen rapid urbanisation and the global population is now expected to grow to more than 8.3 billion by 2050. Currently, 800 million hectares – 38% of the Earth's land surface – is farmed and we'll soon need to give over another 100 million hectares if we continue to use current agricultural methods. That's not additional fertile land that actually exists though, so some are investigating the potential of vertical farming. (page 34)

Boycott

A form of activism in which consumers refuse to buy a product or use a service to protest against unethical practices by the manufacturer/provider.

Biodiversity

The number and variety of organisms found in a specific area. A balanced, healthy ecosystem will support a large number of species, making it rich in biodiversity. Human impact on the environment (for example pollution or deforestation) can reduce biodiversity, causing negative effects on the ecosystem.

Climate change

Climate change describes a global change in the balance of energy absorbed and emitted into the atmosphere. This imbalance can be triggered by natural or human processes. It can cause either regional or global changes in weather averages and frequency of severe climatic events.

Ecosystem

A system maintained by the interaction between different biological organisms within their physical environment, each one of which is important for the ecosystem to continue to function efficiently.

Environment

The complex set of physical, geographic, biological, social, cultural and political conditions that surround an individual or organism and that ultimately determine its form and the nature of its survival.

Global footprint

A person's global footprint refers to the impact that they have on the planet and the people around them, taking into account how much land and water each person needs to sustain their lifestyle.

Global warming

This refers to a rise in global average temperatures, caused by higher levels of greenhouse gases entering the atmosphere. Global warming is affecting the Earth in a number of ways, including melting the polar ice caps, which in turn is leading to rising sea levels.

Infrastructure

The basic, interrelated systems and services needed to underpin a community or society, such as transport and the provision of power and communication systems, as well as public institutions such as schools.

Landfill

A type of waste disposal in which solid waste is buried underground, between layers of dirt. Biodegradable products will eventually break down and be absorbed into the soil: however, non-biodegradable products such as plastic carrier bags will not break down (or will do so very, very slowly).

Pollution

Toxic substances which are released into the environment: for example, harmful gases or chemicals deposited into the atmosphere or oceans. They can have a severe negative impact on the local environment, and in large quantities, on a global scale.

Recycling

The process of turning waste into a new product. Recycling reduces the consumption of natural resources, saves energy and reduces the amount of waste sent to landfills.

Resource consumption

The use of the Earth's natural supplies, including fossil fuels, water, wood, metals, minerals and many others. Growing populations and increased standards of living have resulted in increased consumption of natural resources, which is having a negative effect on the environment.

Sanitation

Usually refers to access to clean drinking water and adequate sewage facilities. Sanitation is the disposal of human sewage. Inadequate sanitation within a community can lead to disease and polluted drinking water.

Sustainability

Sustainability means living within the limits of the planet's resources to meet humanity's present-day needs without compromising those of future generations. Sustainable living should maintain a balanced and healthy environment.

Water scarcity

A lack of access to fresh drinking water. This is often a major problem for communities in regions with very arid climates, such as Sub-Saharan Africa.

Assignments

Brainstorming

⇨ In small groups, brainstorm to find out what you know about sustainability. Consider these questions:

- What do we mean by 'sustainability'?

- Why is achieving a sustainable lifestyle important?

- What is sustainable development?

Research

⇨ Using this book, and the Internet, research the Sustainable Development Goals set by the UN. Choose one of the goals and research why it has been set and what will need to happen in order to achieve it. Write notes on no more than two sides of A4 paper.

⇨ Research the Government's plans for sustainable development in the UK. Write some notes on your findings.

⇨ Friends of the Earth is a charity which promotes environmental sustainability. Visit their website at www.foe.org. What sort of work do they do? List some of their campaigns and achievements.

⇨ Using this book and the Internet, do some research to find out why water is important to sustainable development. Write some notes on your findings and share with your class.

⇨ Research sustainability schemes in London, for example Boris Johnson's plan to utilise disused tube stations and underground networks. Choose your favourite idea and create a presentation that will showcase it to the rest of your class.

Design

⇨ Using the article *What is sustainable food?* on page seven and further research online, brainstorm some ideas for a website that will inform people about sustainable food choices and how they can change their diet to help the planet. Use your ideas to create samples of at least three pages from your website. Remember your site will need a name and a logo.

⇨ Choose one of the articles from this book and create an illustration to accompany it.

⇨ In small groups, imagine you work for a charity that campaigns for encouraging sustainable lifestyles among people in the UK. Plan an event that you could stage in order to raise awareness in your community and encourage people to make changes. Remember that your event should tie in with the ethos of the charity you work for, and create some posters that could be used for promotion.

⇨ In small groups, create an invention that will help to generate energy so that we don't have to rely on fossil fuels. You should draw your invention and annotate it, then share with the rest of your class.

Oral

⇨ Choose one of the illustrations from this book and, with a partner, discuss why the artist chose to depict the issue in this way and your feelings about the cartoon. Share with the rest of your class.

⇨ Create a PowerPoint presentation that explains the steps we can take to achieve a sustainable lifestyle.

⇨ "As a society, we eat far too much meat. Everyone should cut down to just two meat-containing meals per week in order to save the planet." Debate this statement as a class.

Reading/writing

⇨ Read *How do we achieve a sustainable lifestyle?* on page 25 and write a summary for your school newspaper.

⇨ Choose one of the articles in *Chapter 2: Sustainable solutions* and research it further. Write a blog post about your chosen solution.

⇨ Over the course of a week, keep a diary detailing the resources that you use (water, electricity, wood, food, and anything else you can think of). At the end of the week, look back at your diary and think about whether there are any areas where you could cut down the resources you use. Write a summary explaining what you could change in order to achieve a more sustainable lifestyle.

⇨ Write a letter to your headteacher suggesting some changes that your school could make in order to be more sustainable.

⇨ Read *Pavegen introduces pedestrian power in UK's most sustainable building!* on page 38 and write a blog post summarising the article.

⇨ Biodiversity loss is a major concern for many individuals and organisations. But why does the loss of species matter? What effect does it have on the environment? Write an article explaining the impact of biodiversity loss and why it is significant.

Agenda for Sustainable Development 22–3

Agricultural Technologies Strategy 33–4

Amazon rainforest, effect of tree loss 6–7

biodiversity loss 2–3, 20

biological resources for manufacturing goods 28

building-integrated renewable energy generation 27–8

businesses, reducing environmental impact 36

carbon emissions reduction, by businesses 36

carbon footprint 14, 24

cities 17

Centres for Agricultural Innovation 33

cities, sustainability 17

climate, effect of tree loss 6–7

community food growing 31, 32

consumption increase 20–21

crowdfunding, Pavegen 37

Crystal building 38–9

deforestation see tree loss

desalination 28

domestic energy generation 27–8

Earth Overshoot Day 14–15

Ecological Footprint 14

ecological footprint, cities 17

economic development, and water resources 19

economic growth, negative effects 21

ecosystems, and water management 19

energy

from footsteps 37, 38–9

sustainability 27–8

used in food production 8

energy conservation 29

energy storage 27

environmental degradation 4

environmental impact reduction by businesses 36

environmental protection, and water management 19

environmentally friendly products 36

Ethical Eats 32

farming

Agricultural Technologies Strategy 33–4

small farms 12–13

supermarkets' treatment of farmers 30–31

vertical farms 34–5

flexitarian diet 10

flooring, generating energy 37, 38–9

food 11

growing your own 31, 32

improving sustainability 30–32

sustainable 7–8

food waste 7–8, 10

footsteps, generating energy 37, 38–9

Global Footprint Network 14, 15

greenhouse gas emissions

cities 17

and sustainable food 10

growing your own food 31, 32

healthy eating guidelines 9–10

heating 27

homes

energy generation 27–8

improving sustainability 29

reducing carbon emissions 36

human life risk due to environmental degradation 4

innovation to tackle climate change 36

land footprint 24

land shortage, UK 5

lifecycle assessment 26–7

Livewell 2020 Diet 10

Living Planet Index 2

local authorities, support for local food systems 32

local shops

effect of supermarkets 30

supporting 31–2

locally sourced food 10

manufacturing

using sustainable biological resources 28

water usage 24

material footprint 24

measuring lifestyle sustainability 26–7

meat production, raising age of slaughter 10

megafauna loss 20

overshoot 14

Pavegen 37, 38–9

planet overshoot 14

population stabilization 1

poverty, and water management 19

public buildings, reducing carbon emissions 36

renewable energy 27

Siemens, collaboration with Pavegen 38–9

small farms 12–13

social equity, and water management 19

supermarkets 30–31

sustainability 1–2

cities 17

measurement 26–7

personal contributions 29–30

sustainable development 16

Sustainable Development Goals 22–3

sustainable food 7–8, 9–10

sustainable lifestyles 25–30

Sustainable Restaurant Association 32

transpiration 6

transport fuels 27

travel, improving sustainability 29

tree loss 6–7

reducing 36

UK, land shortage 5

UN Agenda for Sustainable Development 22–3

unsustainable growth, consequences 18–19

urban sustainability 17

vertical farms 34–5

waste food 7–8, 10

waste management 28

waste reduction 8, 29–30

water

and food production 8

and manufacturing 24

and sustainability 18–19, 28

water footprint 24

cities 17

zero-carbon homes 36

Acknowledgements

The publisher is grateful for permission to reproduce the material in this book. While every care has been taken to trace and acknowledge copyright, the publisher tenders its apology for any accidental infringement or where copyright has proved untraceable. The publisher would be pleased to come to a suitable arrangement in any such case with the rightful owner.

Images

All images courtesy of iStock, except page 12: SXC, page 16 © Todd DeSantia, page 31 © Neslihan Gunaydin and page 39 © Eric Lagergren.

Icons on pages 3 and 11 are courtesy of Freepik.

Illustrations

Don Hatcher: pages 2 & 26. Simon Kneebone: pages 21 & 37. Angelo Madrid: pages 9 & 34.

Additional acknowledgements

Editorial on behalf of Independence Educational Publishers by Cara Acred.

With thanks to the Independence team: Mary Chapman, Sandra Dennis, Christina Hughes, Jackie Staines and Jan Sunderland.

Cara Acred

Cambridge

January 2016